Cats

By
MARJORIE FARNHAM SCHRODY

GALAHAD BOOKS • NEW YORK CITY

Encore Edition, 1965

Revised Edition © 1960

"Cats in Your Home"

© Copyright, 1957

By Sterling Publishing Co., Inc., New York, N.Y.

This edition published by Galahad Books, New York, N.Y.

This book published with permission of Sterling Publishing

Co., Inc., New York, N.Y.

Library of Congress Catalog Card Number: 73-76738

ISBN: 0-88365-015-0

Printed in the United States of America

CONTENTS

1. Why You Should Have Cats in Your Home

Why should you have a cat or two? There are many good reasons — but most important, cats are likable. They are as comfortable in a furnished room as in a fifteen-room mansion (only you can put more of them into a mansion!).

Cats are clean, the cleanest of all domesticated animals. They do not smell. They are resourceful and more or less accept what comes in life. If you work at night, they adapt their waking hours to fit yours. If you are ill, they spend their time nursing you back to health. If you are bored, they amuse you. If you just want to sit, that suits them to a "T."

Cats like men, women, children, other cats, dogs, almost anything. They like all sorts of food. They like comfort, but they find it almost anywhere. Most cats travel well. They have a minimum of trouble giving birth. They are independent enough to live their own lives, yet affectionate enough to want your company.

Cats come free, or for fabulous prices. And they come in all colors, sizes and temperaments.

There are many ridiculous and false superstitions about cats. Cats do not "suck baby's breath away" or anything of the kind. If a cat is near a baby's face, he is probably being affectionate. Cats don't bother with things they don't like; they just enjoy being close to "their" people.

Cats do not have nine lives. They do have a miraculous faculty for getting themselves out of predicaments, because of their natural resourcefulness and their lithe bodies. Their whiskers act

What is more graceful than a cat? Two cats, of course! These Siamese Seal Points are the aristocrats of the cat world. They have amazing blue eyes with ruby red pupils. All Siamese cats are more desirable if their eyes are almond in shape and slant toward the nose in Oriental fashion.

as feelers and distance gauges. Their supple backbones bend and have elastic cartilage — they are more easily compressed and expanded than human spines. Their stomachs have an automatic "reverse gear" that enables them to regurgitate unsuitable "foods."

They instinctively know about natural poisons — it is man-made hazards to which they succumb.

Cats do not eat rats. However, they will eat mice if they have to. But only hungry cats will eat them, and hungry cats can't catch many, as a cat can't hunt on an empty stomach. Cats, even the best mousers, must have meat — milk and mice are not adequate. Do not get a cat with the idea that since you are mouse-infested, he'll have a full belly all the time. He'll catch more mice faster if he is well fed. A cat with a mousing heritage obviously makes a better mouser than a cat descended from a long line of non-mousers, but it is largely instinctive for any cat to catch mice.

Let me note that a "plain ol' cat" is just as nice, and just as friendly and affectionate as a pure-bred.

A cat is one of the least expensive animals to have for a pet. Generally the initial investment is low — most of the equipment you need, such as dishes, a pan, etc., you will have around the house anyway. Upkeep is low, too — less than a few cents a day.

Cats are graceful and lovely to watch in action. With their natural agility, developed as they pass through kittenhood, they manage to live in a home without breaking your favorite knick-knacks.

Cats are smart and not unfaithful. They do not, and will not, stick with cruel people just for a meal. They must be loved and appreciated to be at their best. They will watch your children, let you know when danger is present, and comfort you when you feel downcast. Make a mistake and they'll tell you about it — but they are quick to forgive.

2. Where and How to Get a Cat

Once you are sure you want a cat, and can give it a good home, you can decide whether you want to take a "free" cat or will buy one, whether you want a particular breed or will take or buy any breed, whether you want a pure-bred pedigreed cat or will take or buy one without a heritage.

If you are going to set your heart on a particular breed or on a high-priced cat, you will undoubtedly have to wait longer and do more searching to get what you want than if you accept a cat from the ASPCA or a friend or buy one from the first pet shop you enter.

"FREE" CATS

The ASPCA usually has cats of all descriptions looking for homes. You won't get a pedigree, but you may be lucky enough to get a pure-bred cat. (Incidentally, a pedigree itself isn't soft and cuddly.) These cats are free, and you may be performing a public service. In fact, if you go out to the shelter and leave a general description of the cat you want, you will be notified when one comes in.

Friends usually have cats. If you get a cat from a friend you will know if the cat has been well taken care of, if his surroundings are clean and neat, and so forth. Friends' cats are usually free cats.

If you live in a rural area, remember that farmers have barns,

Though your cat may have come to you "free," be sure you provide it with a good home. This beautiful Persian Long-hair is a valuable find.

and all barns have cats in excess. No farmer will object to a kitten or two leaving the old homestead. These cats may not be as well fed as house cats and they may have worms, but they will be basically hardy cats and able to endure most conditions. Worms are relatively easy to cure. Barn cats, as a rule, are good mousers.

You may be lucky in obtaining a stray cat. A stray may follow you home, come to your doorstep after a fight, hang around until you invite him in, or maybe not even wait for an invitation. You should be wary not to take someone else's cat, thinking he's a stray. A plump sleek cat, even though he may be out roaming is not a stray — he's almost sure to belong to someone. Cats with collars are, of course, not strays. A stray is a cat without a home, a cat that has been abandoned. If you adopt him, he will either be very grateful or very resentful — no halfway feelings.

Be particularly wary of bringing in a stray if you have kittens or cats in your home already. Your own cats should be vaccinated against feline enteritis first. The stray should be kept secluded until he has been inoculated, and the veterinary has ascertained his health. It is important to bring a stray immediately to the veterinary to minimize infections from any possible contagious diseases.

BUYING FROM A PET SHOP

If there is a pet shop in your vicinity, your search for a cat may be ended. Go in and look around. Talk to the manager — see if he is friendly and willing to please. Do the animals come right up to the doors of their cages when you walk over, or do they run back into a corner? Are their eyes running? Or are they weak-looking?

Proper cleaning, heating and feeding are marks of a good pet shop. If the animals run from people, chances are that somewhere along the line they have been mistreated. When you ask for a price, does the manager give you one, or does he "hem and haw," and feel you out? If the animals look well (pet shop animals never look as well as ones from private homes), and the manager seems honest and trying to please you, then discuss cats.

Pet stores are good for buying pure-bred animals, but be careful. Some pet shops have cats that are not pure-bred, and still sell them for pure-bred prices, either from ignorance or

There is no place like a pet shop for variety of choice in obtaining your cat. You may also want to get your cat a little house to play in, besides the essentials — cat food, toys, medicine — which a pet shop sells.

because "what the buyer doesn't know won't hurt him." Moreover, there have been some cases of faked pedigrees.

You will only get what you pay for. If you definitely want a

It's just as easy to live with two cats as one! They're company for each other and no more trouble for you. They usually share their bed, dishes and toys.

pedigreed animal, don't settle for second best — you will tend to look down on him and you won't be able to give him all the love he needs.

BUYING FROM A BREEDER

The best way to buy a pure-bred cat is directly from the breeder, preferably one in your vicinity (to eliminate shipping). You can get names and addresses from a pet shop, by watching the newspapers, or by going to a cat show and taking down the names of breeders. If you want to buy a cat seen at a show, wait about three weeks so that if the cat has caught anything while being exhibited it will have recovered.

Cats from a breeder will be pedigreed, and you should receive a document stating the pedigree, at the time of purchase. (See Chapter 3 for more about pedigrees.) Sometimes you will not be able to get the pedigree document for a male cat until later — when you produce a certificate from a veterinary saying that you have had him neutered. This protects the breeder from competition from amateurs.

A good cat will not be too cheap — beware of bargains. On the other hand, the cat with the highest price tag isn't always the best either — because of his fancy breeding he may be too high-strung for a family cat. The runt of the litter will be cheapest. Usually females run cheaper than males. If you and a kitten hit it off, get him. You'll both be happier.

No matter where you get your cat, have him checked by a licensed veterinary.

MORE THAN ONE KITTEN?

If you are planning on buying a cat, it is much better to have two. They then have each other for company. Of course, the cat has *you*, but would you like it if you never saw another human? If possible (and it usually is), get litter mates. They are fast friends already, and have no period of adjustment to go through. They are no extra work, and are more than twice the fun.

3. What Kind of Cat?

There are more varieties of cats than pages in this book. The more prominent breeds are the ones we're concerned with here, as the others are too uncommon to warrant mention.

Of all cats, there are two major divisions: Long-hairs and Short-hairs.

PERSIANS

The only accepted and registerable Long-hair in the United States today is the Persian. The Angora, once a breed, is recognized no more. A cat that is sold as Angora may be a half-breed Persian or a faulty Persian.

The Persian is big, with long, thick hair. Because of his massiveness, he is a quiet cat, although a playful kitten. A good Persian's eyes always contrast with his body color — there are thirteen body colors. Persians require more grooming than Short-hairs, but are just as affectionate.

SHORT-HAIRS

The most prominent of the Short-hairs are the Siamese, Domestic Short-hair, Manx, Abyssinian, and Burmese.

SIAMESE — A lithe, svelte smart-as-a-whip devil, the Siamese is guaranteed to be your constant friend and counsellor. Cats are given a color name (such as Seal Point) in accord with the

This dancer is a trained Siamese Seal Point. Siamese cats are generally considered the most desirable breed because of their intelligence and beauty.

color of their "points" — feet, tail, ears and mask. Siamese colors recognized by most shows and cat clubs are: Seal, Chocolate, Blue, and Lilac or Frost Point. Besides these, there are Pink, Red, Orange and Torti (tortoise-shell) Pointed Siamese cats.

Seal Points have deep, dark brown points, and are the most

common. A Seal's body color ranges from cream to a color dark enough to be termed "brown." Chocolate Points are milk chocolate in color, with the body creamy with pinkish-tan noses, (and pink pads on their paws!). Blues have rich blue-gray points, with an icy blue-gray body. The other varieties have cream bodies, and the point colors speak for themselves.

Siamese kittens are born pure white, then gradually change color and gain points as they grow older. They gain full coloring at about one year of age; the coat gets darker and darker until at about five years the coat changes no more. It remains sleek and not the least bit fluffy after the cat leaves the kitten stage.

Siamese are noted for their bright blue, slightly slanted eyes. The body of the Siamese is angular, with a slightly elevated rump set on long, slender hind legs. The feet are small and dainty, the Seal Points having dark pads. The head is wedge-like in shape.

The Siamese are talkative cats, more so than any other breed. Their gutteral squawks will follow you from attic to basement as they continually air their views on life, which some people find annoying. Siamese are noted too for their personality quirks. No two are alike, and no one cat is typical of the breed. Most Siamese like wool, especially wool from garments worn close to the skin, such as gloves, socks, scarves, sweaters, etc. However, their stomach juices can digest small quantities of wool (an animal fiber) with no trouble.

DOMESTIC SHORT-HAIR — Commonly called "alley" cat, this now-recognized breed is rising to its own in the United States. The cat's head is round, with large, round, green, blue or orange eyes. The fur is dense and soft. Color combinations as well as solid colors are accepted in the registry, and any and all colors are available. Tabby (striped or whirled) and Tortoise-shell (yellow, brown and red) are the most common combinations. The breed is hardy, fastidious, and it typifies the word "cat" for many Americans.

MANX — Originally from the Isle of Man, these tailless cats are the most unusual breed. Their hind legs are long and accen-

Two Siamese Seal Point cats.

Standards for all breeds are given fully in the back of this book.

Tortoise-shell and White Persian kittens. The Persian is the only recognized long-haired breed in the United States today. A Tortoise-
shell Persian is a real oddity, and may not be accepted by some cat
associations.

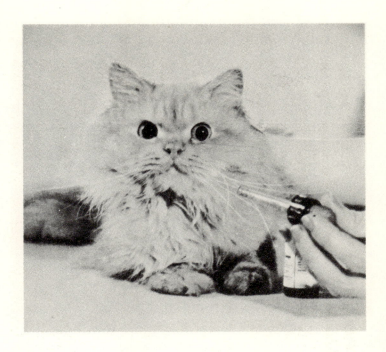

If your beautiful Red Tabby Persian is to have a full coat, you may find it necessary to supplement her diet with vitamins. Some cats will not eat their food if vitamins have been added, and that is why this cat is getting vitamins with an eye dropper.

Standards for all breeds are given fully in the back of this book.

This is a cat without a tail!   The Manx (from the Isle of Man) is famous for its taillessness.   The usual color is Tabby Gray, not Brown, but there are many color varieties.

Standards for all breeds are given fully in the back of this book.

This is a champion Abyssinian. Most cats of this breed are brown, and some are ticked with dark bands spread evenly around the body. Deriving from sacred Egyptian cats, the Abyssinian is noted for its pleasant disposition, aloofness and sweet voice, which it seldom uses.

tuated, and their rumps large and meaty. This causes them to hop instead of walk with grace. A true Manx has a depression where his tail should be. At some shows now we find Manx cats with flat rumps, or just the trace of a first joint. The Manx usually comes in Gray Tabby, although almost all colors can be accounted for. They make gay companions, and are most amusing.

ABYSSINIAN — Descended from Egyptian sacred cats, this breed is very unusual and quite expensive. Their beautiful voices are used infrequently, and so they are among the quietest of cats. Abyssinians are brown, with bands of gray, black and brown spread evenly around their entire body, making them lovely to look at. They are quite playful, and amuse themselves for hours on end.

BURMESE — The Burmese are very similar to the Siamese in body shape, and in character, but are solid brown, with hazel or golden eyes. They are most affectionate, and love playing and people. They are harder to find than the Siamese, but quite a few breeders in this country offer them for sale.

MALE vs. FEMALE

Distinguishing males from females seems to present a problem to the amateur as the male kitten's testicles are not readily noticed. However, if you turn up the kitten's tail and examine its underside (the breeder won't mind) you can reassure yourself as to the gender. The male will have a "colon" (:) while the female will have an "exclamation point" (¡) upside down. This is the easiest way to differentiate, and works quite well.

Whether to get a male or a female is another matter. As kittens, the differences are negligible. Both are cute, playful and adorable, but the males tend to be a little more aggressive. It is when they grow up that you may wish you'd picked either "Susie's cute little brother" or "Tom's cute little sister."

A female makes a better house cat: she will stay in the house if necessary. Also, she will be friendlier, cozier, more affectionate

Regarded by many fanciers as more beautiful than the Siamese is the Burmese. It has many similarities to the Siamese but is more colorful, with a solid seal brown body and yellow or golden eyes. The Burmese is an extremely intelligent cat, but is rare in America now. Most breeders keep their best stock for breeding, and sell off only the less desirable individuals.

Standards for all breeds are given fully in the back of this book.

This is a Tiger Domestic Short-hair, until recently called "alley-cat," but now recognized as a breed and eligible for showing at cat exhibits. The breed includes all varieties from pure white through tortoise-shell to black.

Standards for all breeds are given fully in the back of this book.

Mother and daughter Blue Persian. This cat is noted for its long hair, beautiful copper eyes and squat face. Photograph is by Walter Chandoha. world-renowned photographer.

and quieter around the house (except when she is in heat). When she comes into heat, at about nine months of age, she'll meow, yowl, dash from door to window and back again, and crouch with her tail up. This active stage lasts about a week and occurs from one to eight times a year.

Spaying a female cat is a complex, somewhat costly and difficult operation. It is not dangerous any more, due to modern aseptic surgical techniques. The cat is generally kept hospitalized until ready to go home. After a female is spayed, she will never come into heat, and she will be much, much easier to live with.

A female will be very clean and not get into fights — only cause them! If she goes out, she will have kittens regularly unless you have her spayed. Spaying makes her remain a kitten longer, and does not make her fat and lazy — eating too much and not exercising enough do that. Females are more gentle generally, and not as easily distracted as males.

Toms run bigger and stronger than their sisters, but are no hardier.

A male will never present you with a batch of kittens, but he may be used for stud after one year. A male will not cuddle up as a female does on long evenings. He'd rather be out on the town! A male *has* to go out. If he goes out, he will not mess up the house, but he may stay out for long hours or days at a stretch.

If your male can't go out, he should be neutered (castrated) when he comes of age, which is at about six months. When his testicles drop down fully, have him neutered by your veterinary. This is a simple and inexpensive operation. Your cat will stay at home thereafter, and be a companion instead of a dreamer.

While any cat at all can be housebroken, the unaltered male will "spray." If not neutered, a male will spray (from his anal glands) a musky-smelling liquid into every nook and cranny of your house. The odor is permanent and is made to attract females. A male will also forget his toilet training at times and urinate against the walls, in corners or any place that takes his fancy.

If your neutered cat goes out, he'll come home unscathed and you'll never be bothered by his spraying and yowling. Since a

This Blue Cream Persian kitten is relieving itself in a pan of absorbent clay. The clay holds in offensive odors and eliminates one of the problems of kitten training. The cat's two colors, blue and cream, are well-divided and broken into patches.

Standards for all breeds are given fully in the back of this book.

neutered male presents no problems at all, you may prefer to buy a male kitten if you are not interested in breeding, but merely want to be a cat owner and lover.

PEDIGREES AND REGISTRATIONS

There are five organizations that maintain lists of cats. Their names are:

CAT FANCIERS' ASSOCIATION, INC.
20615 Patton Court
Detroit 28, Michigan
> Sec'y: Mrs. Myrtle K. Shipe

AMERICAN CAT FANCIERS ASSOCIATION
P. O. Box 233
Dallas 21, Texas
> Sec'y: Russell Middleton

AMERICAN CAT ASSOCIATION
1710 Wesley Avenue
Evanston, Illinois
> Sec'y-Treas.: Mrs. Stanley Gibson

CAT FANCIERS FEDERATION
1150 Bedford Street
Stamford, Connecticut
> Sec'y: Mrs. Ralph A. Wilkinson

THE UNITED CAT FEDERATION, INC.
737 Butterfield Road
San Anselmo, California
> Sec'y: W. F. Jack Wedel

These organizations maintain lists of registered cats. Once a cat is registered, its pedigree may be kept in their books. The cat may be registered with one or all of these associations.

The pedigree is the chart of a cat including its name and breed with as much of its ancestry as the owner knows. The

This Silver Tabby Domestic Short-hair has made itself comfortable in a favorite armchair, a trick most cats pick up fast enough without any help from a trainer. The tabby markings are obvious in this specimen, but in some cats of the same breed and color, the markings may be very confused.

association sends a form for registration to each cat owner applying. The information on the registration form will include age, sex, date of birth, coloring, description of all sorts, its mother and father, owner, breeder, and ancestry. If the ancestry is unknown, you can simply state "Unknown" in the proper place.

Each of these associations also maintains a Foundation Record. This is for cats who have a known ancestry for three or four generations. The ancestors must also have been included in the

This little ball of fur is a Cream Persian kitten. The scratching post has a piece of catnip on the end of the spring on top of the post, which the cat is trying to get. In her efforts she keeps her nails trimmed, has loads of fun and gets plenty of exercise.

Standards for all breeds are given fully in the back of this book.

Notice how this Tortoise-shell Domestic Short-hair loves being brushed
—and so do all cats! When brushing your cat (see page 54) begin
gently until your cat gets to know you and the routine. Brushing
regularly keeps him from shedding hairs all over the house, and it
makes his coat shiny, bright and clean.

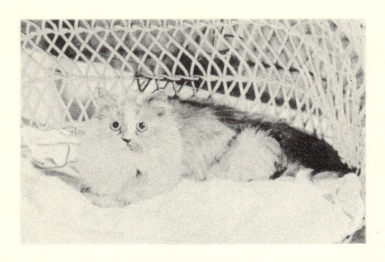

This is a beautiful young Shaded Silver Persian, much lighter in color than a Blue, shading from dark on the ridge to white on chin, chest, belly and legs, as the standards require. This champion has a bed of his own, as all good cats deserve, even if the bed is only a cardboard box.

Stud Book. The offspring of cats who have been registered in the Stud Book for three or four generations are automatically included.

Almost any cat today is a so-called "pure breed," as Domestic Short-hair is considered a breed by the various associations. A number of cats that have been winning championships are strays in the class of Domestic Short-hairs. Since Domestic Short-hairs became a breed, there is a great deal of confusion in the showing and registering of cats. All other breeds such as Siamese, Manx, etc., should have papers for show purposes as only those cats with a pure bloodline in those classifications can be recorded.

4. Your New Kitten

FEEDING

If you have a mother cat, she'll take care of the whole feeding process, right up to meat eating. She'll watch what the kittens eat, how much and when. She'll teach them to lap up milk, teach them which foods are good, and teach them not to touch spoiled food.

Little kittens up to four months of age, should, if their mother is running out of milk, be given small supplementary feedings of a warmed milk mixture as often as they need it. About twice a day should be enough; if the mother is completely dry, every four hours. Mix one egg with a day's ration of half evaporated milk and half water. Until the kittens are about two months old, the mother will be gradually weaning them with bits of her own food.

If your kittens were old enough to leave their mother when you got them, then you shouldn't have much of a problem. The only questions will be how many times a day and how much you need to feed them. If the mother cat is not around, keep feeding the kittens milk *only* until their first teeth appear. Then about four times a day give them each a teaspoonful of tinned cat food, or grated meat, or baby food, with two teaspoonsful of the egg-and-milk mixture.

Mother Siamese instructs her china youngster, while the photographer (versatile George Pickow) manages to snap the shutter in time.

As your kittens get older, give each a couple of tablespoonsful of solid food at a feeding, about four feedings a day. If this is impossible, give them a little more food, and feed them no less than three times. Milk and egg mixed up together for breakfast; baby food, beef or cat food for luncheon; and milk and egg plus cat food for supper, would comprise a decent diet. When the kittens are over six months old, feed them twice a day; when a year old, one feeding a day will do (although two feedings are preferable).

KITTEN'S NEW HOME

After eight weeks, a kitten, of any breed but Siamese, may be taken from his mother into his new home. (Siamese stay kittens for a long time. Even though their eyes open the earliest of any of the breeds, they are slower, physiologically, to develop. Siamese are excellent mothers, and usually have an abundant supply of milk. A Siamese can be removed from his mother when three months old.)

When you first get the kitten, put him down and let him alone. Don't give him anything to eat, except a small bowl of water where he can see it. And show him where his pan is.

He probably won't have a bowel movement for twelve hours or so; or he may be rushing to the pan every few minutes. This is caused by his nerves and the transition, and is considered a normal condition. He may have to urinate, and probably frequently. This will accustom him to his new pan. If he is very frightened, and makes a mess on the floor, *do not* punish him. He will be too scared to understand, and you will only make matters worse. Move him to his sleeping box (see Chapter 6) and calmly clean up the mess. There is no sense in putting him in his pan now, because he no longer needs it. Do that the next time! (See Chapter 6 on TOILET TRAINING).

When nighttime comes, your little kitten will probably cry. If he is a Siamese, you won't get any sleep. If he is of another breed, you may be able to sleep if you are hard-hearted. For all concerned, it is a good idea to move the kitten's box near your bed. (You can put him in bed with you, but once a cat sleeps on a bed, it is the start of a lifelong habit. He will want to curl up with you ever after.) If you put the box by the bed, you can reach a hand down and comfort your kitten. Or, you can wrap a hot water bottle in a towel and put it in the box, *flat under the cat.* If you stand it up, it may fall down and suffocate the kitten. A ticking clock has been said to help, as it simulates the mother cat's heartbeat and is a constant, reassuring noise.

Bear in mind that no cat, especially a kitten, will behave in his new home as he did when you picked him out. At times, the first few days can be very discouraging. Koki, one of our Siamese queens, was as sweet as pie while with her mother, but the minute she set paw inside our door she was vicious. After a week of love and affection we could approach her without being forced to wear leather gloves. Now she is one of our most affectionate cats, and loves one and all.

Your newly-located kitten is frightened and lonesome. He is trying hard to learn where his pan, food and bed are, and to familiarize himself with the surroundings. Give him a day or two (generally) and he'll act as though he owns the place.

Limit his surroundings to one or two rooms, or a small area, when you first bring him home. It will keep him from getting "lost," and help his (and your) peace of mind. After he is familiar with you, then let him explore the house. Go with him the first time, just in case he gets into something he can't get out of. He won't be happy until he has gone over every nook and cranny with a fine tooth comb! Then, after he is acclimated, he'll be safer and happier.

If the kitten is going to be an indoor-outdoor cat, don't let him out until he is sure of himself in the house. Go with him the first two or three times he goes out — until he gains his sense of direction and knows where the door is.

The second morning your kitten is with you he should be hungry. He'll eat, explore and get into mischief. Once he has broken bread with you, however humble the fare, he will be your buddy.

Give him a small dishful of milk as his first feeding in new territory. Warm it by adding hot water, but if it is too hot he'll burn his mouth. Test it on your wrist, as you would for an infant. After the initial feeding, you can start right in feeding him meat, fish, or canned cat and dog food.

VITAMINS

Supplements of vitamins, especially Vitamin D and the B vitamins, should be added to a kitten's diet at any early age. Vitamin D is a preventative for rickets, a disease prevalent in kittens, especially those fed on a diet of only canned food. (More on rickets in Chapter 8.)

Cow's milk that you use should be the Vitamin D type; evaporated milk usually has this vitamin. Bone meal is quite inexpensive, and should be mixed in with all the food until the

After your kitten is in his new home for a day, he will begin to explore and get himself into mischief. Every cat has the ability to balance, tread softly and some even can walk around the most delicate crystalware without knocking any over!

cat is at least eight months old. Make sure it is *steamed* bone meal.

Brewers yeast tablets, another necessary supplement, may be purchased at pet shops or drug stores. Start feeding the kitten these after his teeth come in. Your kitten should have one tablet a day until he is about three months old; then one and one-half tablets until he is about eight months old; give him two tablets per day thereafter. Most cats love these, and eat them with no coaxing. They make a nice reward, too, when you are teaching your cat skills. If he won't eat them, grind them up and mix them in his food.

Cod liver oil, the kind given to babies, should also be given to your cat. Cats and kittens will lap this right up with no trouble because of its fishy smell and taste. Your veterinary will be able to tell you the dosage for your particular cat.

Therefore, a diet of Vitamin-D-added milk, fresh meat, yeast tablets, as well as canned foods, plus any other supplements your veterinary advises, will insure your growing kitten against most nutritional defects. A healthy cat will fight germs better, and he'll stay a well cat!

Cats must have a balanced diet. If your cat is to have a beautiful coat and is to develop mentally and physically in the proper way, it may be necessary to supplement his diet with vitamins and minerals. This Siamese was very sick until he started getting vitamin supplements.

5. Feeding Cats

Feeding a grown cat is much easier than feeding a little kitten. Kittens must be fed frequently, fed only certain things, and are generally either little pigs or abstainers! Cats can be fed less often, can eat less specialized food, and will eat as they need it.

A grown cat should be fed twice a day. Fresh water should always be available, as cats need water and drink it frequently. A grown cat develops his own eating habits. He may like fruit, vegetables, or almost anything. Just because he likes a food, though, is not the reason for selecting it.

BONES, MEAT AND MILK

Technically, a cat should have fresh meat, milk and a hard bone to chew on. The bones should be chicken *heads* only, large bones from beef and veal, and lamb bones. Fish bones, steak and chop bones, and any bones from the pig (pork) are extremely dangerous as they will splinter and choke a cat, or puncture his intestines.

Fresh meat is rather an expensive commodity for the house pet, unless you buy stewing beef. Many of the tinned cat and dog foods are good and nourishing, and cats seem to like most of the flavors. However, a cat's teeth are for tearing and gnawing, and the tinned food must be supplemented with an occasional bone, dog biscuit or fresh meat.

Horsemeat, fresh or tinned, is fine, but not for a steady diet as it hasn't enough fat and your cat may develop eczema.

Milk is liquid meat to a cat. Most cats will drink a lot of milk, but milk alone is no diet for a cat. Instead of fresh milk, you can use evaporated milk mixed with an equal part of water (warm water if the milk is refrigerated). This is just as nourishing and tasty, and much cheaper in price. Cream is a luxury, fattening and extremely rich. Cats have been known to break out from too much cream. But most cats like it, and if you can afford it, there is no reason why your cat can't have some now and then as a treat.

Hamburger for cats is pointless. First of all, a cat would rather grind his own meat. Then too, other meats are cheaper, and hamburger is too fatty. Kidneys of all kinds are generally enjoyed by cats. Heart tastes delicious to cats, too, and is generally inexpensive. About the cheapest fresh meats are brains and lungs. Cats from all walks of life really go for them. If you can't stand the sight of these, give the cat the package as it comes from the butcher. He'll tear it open with ease. But, if you do this, you run the risk of having a trail of meat blood and juice throughout your house.

STARCHES AND FATS

Don't give your cat an excess of fat or gravy. The only table scraps you should give him are meat, gristle and muscle, but weed out the fat. A *little* gravy or a *little* fat won't harm him. Gravy is not advisable because of the flour that goes into it. Pan gravy, if not too greasy, is fine, and cats seem to think so too!

Starches aren't good for cats, as cats have no way of assimilating carbohydrates. Cats will eat bread, potatoes, and other starches, sometimes for the taste, or sometimes because they are very hungry. Pandora will sneak up on the table and steal bread any time she finds some. She'll drag it furtively under the table, nibble one corner, and then sneak back for more. "Stolen fruits taste sweetest" even to a cat.

VEGETABLES

Some cats eat vegetables, and other cats would eat vegetables if they had them. Grass is about the only vegetable a cat *should* eat. Generally, green leafy vegetables in a limited amount won't do your cat any harm. Cooked carrots won't either. But don't feed him lima beans, corn, peas and starchy vegetables. Don't give him any, even if he assures you they are the only thing he wants. He'll settle for a dab of milk instead.

Spicy foods are not for cats. Most of my own cats have a passion for ravioli. The minute they smell it, they come leaping up onto the table and steal it from under my very nose! I usually let them have a drop or two of the sauce, and then shoo them away. I don't let them lick out the plates (even when they tell me how cruel and heartless I am), because there is too much sauce there. It is hard to resist plaintive "meows" and starved stares, but it is even harder to nurse a sick cat!

CANNED FOODS

Some of the canned *dog* foods will stick to the roof of a cat's mouth, as they are prepared for gulping dogs, not nibbling cats. If you feed your cat canned foods, give him a little milk in a separate dish, for washing down the food when necessary.

After your cat has grown up, give him eight ounces of meaty food a day, in either one or two feedings. With canned food, this amounts to about a quarter of an average can per twice-a-day serving. Do not buy the very cheap tinned foods. It is worth a few more cents to make sure your cat is getting the vitamins and nutritious elements he needs.

Read the can's label carefully. Be sure the food isn't too high in calcium and ash. Make certain the can shows a statement of registry with a department of agriculture, is guaranteed by a

Cats are not usually finicky eaters. Do not feed your cat such vegetables as beans, corn or peas. Do feed him a balanced canned food if you have no suitable table scraps.

known agency, or (if these are not required in your state) at least shows an analysis of the contents. Be sure that you buy reputable brands.

Canned fish food is generally more appealing to cats than canned meat food, except for pure horsemeat. Fish is very good for cats. With fresh fish you must first cook and bone the fish, as small bones are deadly.

EGGS

Your cat should have one raw egg a week, for nutritional purposes, and also to give his coat a glossy sheen. The eggs may be mixed with his milk, or given to him "straight." After a few months of this, you will notice a decided improvement. His fur will be softer and silkier to the touch, an indication it is healthy and "alive." Most cats like raw eggs, particularly in milk.

DISHES AND EATING HABITS

Your cats should have their own set of dishes and these should be thoroughly washed after each meal. Don't leave food sitting in them; pick them up about twenty minutes after the cats have stopped eating. This gives them time to come back, if they decide they want more. If you leave food down all the time, the cats will spoil their appetite, and the food will smell and get rancid. All you should leave down for them is fresh water, with milk if you desire, and an occasional bone or cat biscuit as a treat. Be sure your cats' dishes are well rinsed, as they do not like soapy food any more than you do.

Try to feed your cats at approximately the same hour every day. Cats are creatures of habit, and get hungry at regular intervals. They'll be healthier with regular feedings, and less likely to gorge themselves.

Some cats are problem eaters . . . they don't like this, something else gives them a rash, etc., etc. With this kind of eater, if it isn't a matter of tastes, it is advisable to take him to a competent veterinary, who will perhaps give him tests, and give you a few feeding suggestions. If it is a matter of likes and dislikes, the easy way out is, of course, to follow the line of least resistance and feed the cat what he likes (provided it won't harm him). Otherwise, put down his regular food, at the regular time. If he just sniffs at it, and strolls off he might not be hungry. Perhaps he caught a mouse, or just lost his appetite prior to a cold. Pick his food up and preserve it for the next meal. If your cat won't

In this picture you can see the rumps of two and heads of three different kinds of Siamese cats (Seal Point, Blue Point and Chocolate Point, in that order from left to right). You can also see the way a hungry cat eats.

eat his dinner, but scratches at the floor, trying to cover it up, he wants something better, or the food might be tainted.

If your cat won't eat the same kind of food for three days, and the food is neither spoiled nor rancid, and you know he hasn't been getting any other food, try him on just plain milk. Do not give him a favorite delicacy now, as his stomach has shrunk and if he eats a lot he will have an upset stomach. If he won't eat at all, take him to your veterinary, as he may be coming down with something more serious than a cold.

Most cats like baby food. It is especially good for old cats whose teeth have departed, and for very young kittens. Expensive, but nourishing, it can be mixed with dog meal and water, which brings the price down and stretches the meat.

If your cat watches you eating steak, when he has a dish of milk in front of him, don't be surprised if he thinks you are a cruel monster. If he can't cajole you out of a morsel or two, and he can't steal any, he'll probably give you a killing look, then sit and sulk. My conscience won't let me eat steak without sharing. One look at my cats — even though I know the swaying from "starvation," half-closed eyes, weak little cries, and all the rest, are an act — and I cut off a little bit of steak for them. This is enough. They don't (usually!) want to rob me; they just want a taste. Then they go back to their milk, and I can eat in peace. Sometimes it's worth it.

6. Care

Cats *can* get along with no care at all from humans. They may also leave an otherwise happy home because of too much coddling. Generally, cats love attention though, and the more you give your cats, the friendlier they will be.

Cats enjoy love, and lots of it. They don't care if you love them in a hut or a palace, and care not whether they eat from tin dishes or bone china. They don't care about your background, or your job, so long as you have time for them. They'll adjust their hours to yours, and alter their mealtimes to suit your convenience so long as the feedings are regular.

THE CAT'S BED

Each cat and kitten should have his own box . . . a place where he can be alone to think and sleep, or do whatever cats do in their off moments. A cardboard carton, with one side cut down for accessibility, padded with an old, clean towel or a doll- or baby-blanket will make a cat as happy as a special cat basket bought in a pet shop. This is his domain. You can remove the padding to wash it, as long as you put in a substitute. When your cat is in there, he wants privacy. When he wants company he will come and seek you out.

Cats need sunshine, exercise and affection. These two people are wise in bringing their cats outside on leashes where they can relax in the sun and chew on some grass.

HOT AND COLD

Cats like it warm, and cats can stand heat better than most animals. If you have radiators, a piece of plywood over the top of one will give them a warm place to sit. Your cats may curl up on the register, or in front of a space heater. Cats take changes in temperature well, too . . . from inside to outside and back again. Generally your cats will catch a cold only from a draft or a drastic temperature change — that is, if they are indoor cats and get out on an extremely cold day. But, most of the time cats run in the snow, then come and curl up by the hottest place in the house with no ill effects.

WET AND DRY

Cats like it dry, too. There are, of course, exceptions. Pandora loves to curl up in the bathroom sink with the water running, and Coquette will jump into the bathtub whenever she hears splashing. However, neither of them venture outdoors in the slightest drizzle! If your cats or kittens have been outside in the rain and come back soaking wet, it is best to towel them dry

Cats love company . . . even their own company. They snuggle together when sleeping, and generally have a good time all by themselves.

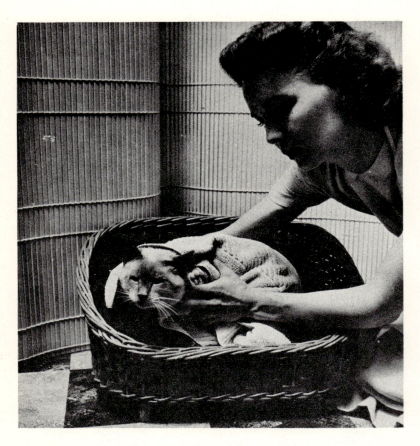

If your cat gets wet and it is cold outside, dry the cat off as thoroughly as possible, wrap him in a heavy towel and put him to bed. Cats can catch cold and when they do it may be serious.

and let them finish off the job by licking. The toweling will make the job easier for them, and start their blood circulating faster to help prevent a chill. They should be kept out of drafts, but they will probably see to this themselves.

LIFTING

The correct way to lift up *any* cat is with two hands . . . *never* by the scruff of the neck, and never by the stomach alone, or by front legs, tail, etc. Put one hand under the cat's chest and stomach, and use the other to support his feet.

Lift your cat with two hands!

HOUSEBREAKING

Cats are the easiest of domestic animals to housebreak. Generally you won't even have to go through this phase. If a kitten has been with its mother for any length of time, she has taken care of it for you.

Most cats and kittens are trained to an indoor pan. A large enameled pan, such as a roasting pan, or dish pan, with sides low enough for the kitten to jump over and see above, is all you need. Also on the market are inexpensive disposable waxed pans of heavy cardboard. The pan may be filled with dirt, moss, odor-absorbing earths or shavings, but never sawdust or sand, as the cat will get particles in his paws, eyes, and fur (and consequently into his stomach), to say nothing of tracking it all over the house. There are products on the market now, which are chemically treated to prevent odors and to attract cats to them.

The pan should either be sifted or changed every day, as cats don't care to use a dirty pan any more than you like one around. If the pan gets too dirty, the cat may use the floor or the rug as a not-too-subtle hint for you to clean up.

If your cat is not trained to use a pan when you first get him, show him where it is, and then take his paws in your hand and make digging motions with them until you have dug a little hole. Then sit him on it. If he doesn't have to use it then, he will at least get the idea. Don't move the pan about without making sure your cat knows where it is. This safeguards against accidents. Every week or so scrub the pan out with a brush and hot, soapy water. Don't use a strong disinfectant, because it may be toxic to cats, and the slightest trace of smell will repel him. Use a detergent or a soap, or just put water in the pan and boil it on the stove. This prevents germs and bacteria from developing, and helps to keep the pan clean and sweet-smelling for you and your cat.

A couple I know had a Manx cat, Tau, who would go outside, and then scratch on the screen to come in again. When let in, he would run to his pan, use it, and then ask to go out again.

They kept moving the pan nearer and nearer to the door, and finally put it outside, then dispensed with it altogether and let Tau use the great outdoors, which never needs emptying.

If you try to train a kitten to torn-up newspapers in his pan, he may play in it. Newspaper is unnatural, and too fluttery — it distracts a kitten. Of course, if you persist, he'll use it, but unhappily.

If you decide eventually to let your kitten or cat go outside to perform his daily duties, it is best to go out with him the first few times and show him a patch of dirt, and dig his claws in it for him, so he'll realize the purpose of the trip.

A cat will never dirty his sleeping box, or any place else that is "his domain." Cats are naturally clean animals.

If you do not clean your cat he will clean himself!

GROOMING

Your cat should be brushed every day if he is a short-hair, twice a day if a long-hair, and more frequently in the fall and spring when he is changing coat and shedding a lot. Brushing helps *you* by leaving less hair for him to shed on the furniture. It helps the cat, because when he licks himself he swallows hair

It's easy to advise that you brush your Long-hair twice a day, but do you have time? People who are interested in showing their cats must find the time to groom them daily.

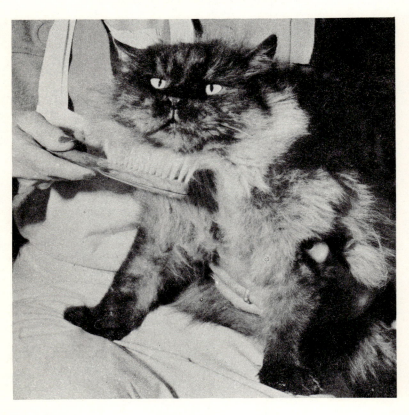

54

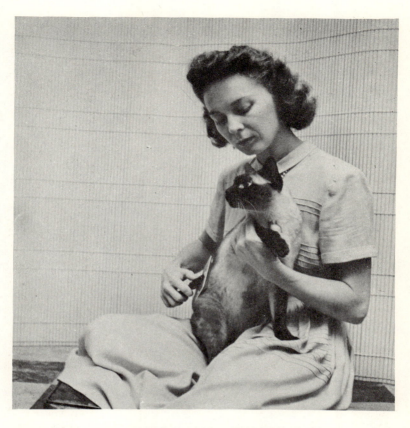

Even short-haired cats like Siamese, must be groomed daily. It's easier to brush loose hairs from a cat than from a chair.

and this invites the danger of hair balls (discussed more fully in Chapter 8).

Most cats like to be brushed, although some don't want their stomachs or chests touched and, in protest, will dig you with their hind feet. Start brushing your cat regularly from the time you get him. Cats like routine and enjoy sitting in your lap and getting stroked. Tomcats may not like to have their fur brushed upward. With long-hairs, it is advisable to brush the fur both ways, as the soft undercoat sheds too, and by brushing in all directions you get more hair out. If your cat is shedding quite a lot, rub a damp cloth on him to help remove the excess hairs.

It is not necessary to buy a special brush; these are usually designed for dogs and are too stiff and large for a kitten or small cat. Brushes of the type used to apply polish to shoes with a small round clump of bristles on one end, will work admirably. These are soft, and thick enough to get a lot of hair out, yet small enough to get under the chin, on top of the head, etc. Use a different brush for each cat, and clean the brushes frequently. Pull the hair out of the brush after each grooming session and every two weeks or so wash the brush in warm water to get the dirt off. This will keep your cat from leaving dark spots on light-colored upholstery or bedspreads.

BATHING

Cats keep themselves fairly clean; they "bathe" all the time. But then there are cats like Regal Prince (Siamese) who washes, and washes, and washes . . . but always the same paw! If he gets dirty, he lets one of his playmates take care of that! Most cats will, after you've spent time brushing them, walk away in disgust and give themselves a *good* "bath," with contempt in their eyes for human means.

If a cat should get really dirty, from coal dust, mud or the like, it may be necessary to give him a bath. Bathing a cat should not be done often, as it dries out the natural oils in his skin. Moreover, most cats don't care for the process.

If you must bathe your cat as a last resort, then put a few inches of warm, clear water in your bathtub or kitchen sink. Put a dish towel or rubber mat in the bottom so the cat will have something other than your arms to dig his claws into. Use a mild detergent or soft soap. Wet him all over, except his head, being careful not to splash any water on his face or into his ears. Then,

Cats usually do not like baths and they do not need to be bathed often as they are perpetually bathing themselves. This is the correct way to bathe your cat . . . keeping the water away from his face.

starting at the neck, either pour on a small amount of the detergent, or make a soap lather, and start rubbing it down his backbone, from the neck to the base of the tail. Gradually work around his sides, and to his stomach, legs and paws, doing his

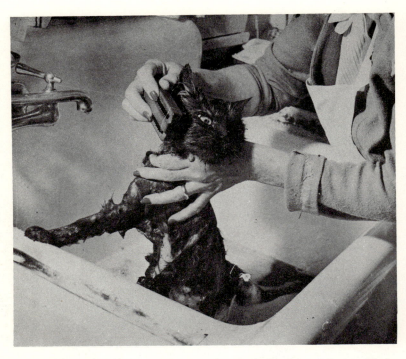

The WRONG way. Do not get too ambitious with the bath. Scrubbing a cat's ear with a brush is not a good idea—especially if the cat scratches you in self-defense. Remember that his ears are very sensitive, not only to noise, but to the touch. If you must clean your cat's ears use cotton and not a scrubbing brush.

tail last. If his face is very dirty, work down from the top of his head.

Be very careful not to get soap or water into his eyes, nose, mouth or ears. If you are fortunate enough to have a double sink, it simplifies matters, as you can then lift him to the other sink into clear water. Otherwise, hang on to him well, lift him out

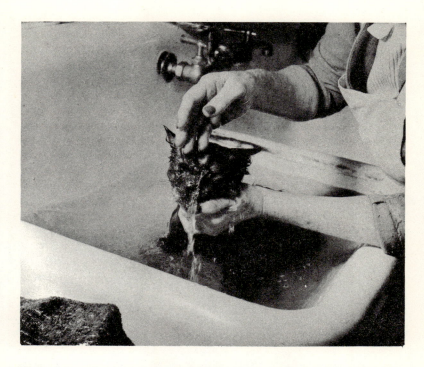

Wrong! A cat's eyes are as sensitive to soap and water as your own. Don't be cruel in bathing your cat. Keep his head dry. Do not allow any soap or water to enter your cat's eyes as it will only make him uncomfortable and bring tears to his eyes.

of the sink (lest he become frightened at the water draining out) and change the water. It should be necessary only to rinse him twice, but do make sure that all the soap comes out of his fur.

When he is clean again, towel him well, and calm him down in your lap while you are rubbing him off. He may claw you, and favor you with dirty looks galore, but he'll soon forget the

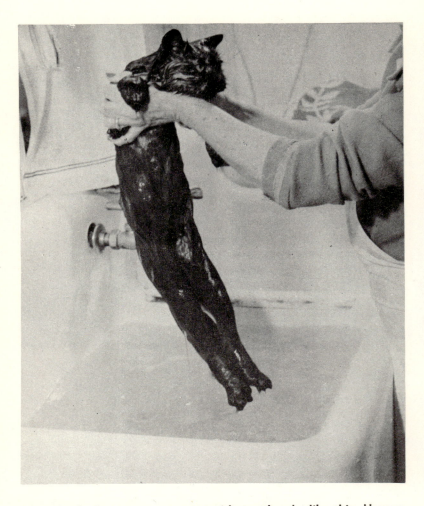

After the bath, remove your cat with two hands, like this. Have a large, extra-heavy towel ready to dry him off. If you first lift a wet cat out of the bath and then go looking for a towel the cat will make a dash for a hiding place.

In drying off your cat, use one hand to hold the cat in the towel and the other to rub him dry. If you let the cat go for an instant, he will attempt to shake himself dry and this will get you and everything around the cat saturated with water. Keep your cat warm after you've dried him. If you have an electric hair dryer then use that to get all the excess moisture from his coat.

humiliation. If you see in the beginning that your cat is going to put up a fight, either wear old heavy gloves, or put him in a pillow case and wash him through that. He won't like it, but it may save you from getting clawed.

All cats love warm wooly toys. What did kittens do before the invention of yarn? Give a kitten a ball of yarn or string and he will keep himself occupied until he is mature.

PLAYTHINGS

All cats like toys. Old spools or balls of yarn will do nicely. Some kittens like soft cuddly toys, others like harder chewy ones, and Siamese often prefer a discarded woolen. You can make a sock doll from an old woolen sock. Stuff the mate of the outside sock in the toe and then tie it with a bit of yarn in the middle to make your cat a comfy and acceptable play toy.

Kittens and cats like catnip . . . dried, in "mouse" form, or as a fresh herb from the garden or flowerpot. A cat or kitten with a catnip mouse is amused (and amusing) for hours. He'll toss it, run after it, pounce on it, lick it, and have loads of fun and mousing experience.

My cats like ping-pong balls better than spools, because they roll in any direction at all. Pet stores handle toys of all kinds. For a slight bit of change you can keep your cat quite happy.

SCRATCHING POSTS

Not in a class with either toys or grooming is the scratching post. This is a small log, with the bark left on, nailed to a square

Here is a different kind of scratching post from the carpet-covered kind shown on page 30. This has the natural bark left on it. Some posts have both bark and burlap or rug.

board that is big enough for the cat to sit on. Sometimes the base is covered with carpeting. You can easily make one of these, or buy one. The pet store variety is usually well sprinkled with oil of catnip to attract the cat initially to it. However, this is generally not needed, as the outdoor smell of the stump itself should suffice. This log, or scratching post, is a definite necessity for you and the cat, particularly if you keep your cat indoors most of the time. If he learns to sharpen his claws on the post you won't have tattered rugs or torn upholstery, and it will keep his nails trim.

Show your cat where the post is and how to claw. Induce him to claw, either by putting his front feet on the post, or by lifting him up and letting him grab onto it with all four feet. This will give him the idea. Then every time you see him digging your rugs or furniture, bring him to his post and help him use it. In a very short time he'll learn, and chances are he'd rather use the post anyway, as it is firmer and "woodsier."

The scratching post is wonderful for your cat's muscle tone and keeping him fit. He'll do his daily calesthenics there with no urging and be very amusing in the process.

NAIL CARE

If your cat goes outdoors alone, his nails should never be cut at all, as they aid him in climbing and are his only defense against other animals. The climbing he does will keep them trim.

If you have an indoor cat, and you have provided him with a scratching post, there should be no need ever to have his claws trimmed.

Occasionally, a cat's nails need trimming. If a cat's nails grow too long, they will hurt. If you try to clip them yourself, without the proper training and tools, the nail may split, or you may accidentally cut down to the quick. It is best to let a competent veterinarian take care of this.

Cat scratching posts come as expensive as your pocketbook can afford. This is a luxurious post filled with catnip. Catnip makes cats go into ecstacy and they rub and scratch and keep their nails trim.

COLLARS

Collaring cats is a much disputed subject. If a cat runs outdoors a lot, a collar can be, and often is, very dangerous. But if you have an "apartment cat" or a female that is kept mostly indoors, a properly fitted collar is fine.

Collars on outdoor cats do serve the purpose of telling "cat-wanters" that this cat belongs to someone and is not a stray. If there is any identification on the collar, you stand a better chance of having your cat returned if he gets lost.

As for bells on collars, they are purportedly for the purpose of warning birds that a cat is coming. Any self-respecting bird knows this anyway, and most of the birds that cats catch are enfeebled or careless. Bells *will* frighten away mice and rats, but, whose side are we on? Cats are mousers, so why hinder them? There are people who get a cat to de-mouse their place, then bell the cat!

Collars on outdoor cats are a hindrance in fighting. Also, many cats have been strangled while climbing trees — they slip and the collar catches over a branch. Some people advise collars with elastic backs, as the cat can slip the collar over his head and jump free, if he gets caught. These collars have a drawback however, as they are useless in training a cat to the leash — when you pull the leash the collar slips off.

A cat that is going to be leash trained (covered in Chapter 7 in detail) has to wear a collar some of the time. The more he wears it the sooner he gets used to it. If you're going to bother to leash train your cat, he won't be running loose much anyway.

Round leather collars, or collars with soft felt backing are best, as a collar tends to wear away the hair on a cat's neck, eventually. If you get a flat collar, get a very narrow one. All cat collars should be light in weight.

The collar should not be so tight that it hinders the cat when he eats, nor so loose that he accidentally catches his lower jaw in it while washing. If he should get his jaw caught, throw a jacket or towel over him to stop his thrashing about, then take

Cats can be taken out on a collar or harness and leash. If your cat is a stranger to the neighborhood, it is a wise idea to walk him all about the vicinity of your home so he won't get lost if he gets out of the house by accident.

off the collar, cutting it if necessary. Calm him down, and (if possible) put the collar back on him, one hole tighter than it was before.

Check your *kitten's* collar every week and a half. A collar that is "just right" in size one day may suddenly be outgrown, as kittens grow at an astounding rate.

Almost any cat will accept a collar without much of a fuss. At first, your cat may try to claw it off, but he soon will forget he has it on. Some cats (the showmen of the race) love a collar and parade around with it. If you tie a bow on the collar they strut all the higher. Most cats, however, are annoyed by a bow and will take measures to claw one off.

Choke collars for cats are totally uncalled for. In theory they seem to be perfect: (1) the pressure is applied only when the cat pulls, and lets up the minute the cat stops pulling; (2) when the cat is not on the leash, the collar hangs free and doesn't rub off the fine neck fur; (3) if the cat is caught on a tree, the collar will slip off over the cat's head; (4) since it works not by pulling but by choking, the cat is supposed to learn to walk on the leash better and faster; ad infinitum. But, this is sadly not the case. A cat is a stubborn, independent animal. He will choke himself to death before he will be pulled where he doesn't wish to go. When a cat pulls an ordinary collar, it will not choke him, but will drag him, thereby eliminating all chance of accident. Also, if a cat gets his leash wrapped around something, as cats are prone to do, there is no danger of a slow and agonizing death with an ordinary collar.

"Poppit bead" collars that snap apart are good for outdoor cats, but not on leashes.

Flea collars are practical in theory, and are comparatively safe. But they must be frequently replaced.

There are harnesses sold which have been built especially for cats. Their only major disadvantage is that they may cause kittens to become bowlegged, if worn all the time. However, they do eliminate all danger of choking and of sore necks. Many times a cat who won't walk on a leash when collared, will respond with no trouble to a harness. They are best used on adult cats.

7. Training

Training your cat to any more than cleanliness (which is inherent) requires the patience of Job plus a lot of time. Your cat will understand you, but being his own independent self, he will obey as he sees fit, which is not very often.

Before meals is an excellent time to teach a cat a skill, as dinner proves a suitable reward. As for "household commands" — "no-no," "down," etc. — your cat will learn these and obey them if he sees that you really mean business. Constant repetition of the commands and an occasional spank on the rump with a rolled-up newspaper will help him learn not to jump on tables or other places where he is not wanted.

"SIT UP"

Almost any cat will "sit up" for his dinner, if it is held within reach, above his head, and the words "sit up" are repeated. His natural impulse *is* to reach up for it, and soon he will associate the words with the deed, and sit up on command at any time.

RETRIEVING

An English authority on cats had only one that would retrieve. If she threw a woolen ball, the cat would bring it back to be thrown again. This cat was a "natural" retriever, her mistress wrote.

I had one cat who would retrieve small sticks. Frisky was a neutered short-hair, about six months old. At the time, I was teaching Tammy, a Collie pup to retrieve, and since the dog proved slow to learn, Frisky would bring me a stick to throw. I'd toss it, and then he would patiently try to teach Tammy. Or when I'd throw a stick to Tammy, and he would just sit and look at me, the cat would finally go get it and show it to Tammy. He never did manage to teach the dog, but he got a lot of fun and exercise in the attempt.

A friend of mine has a Siamese neuter a year old who retrieves, but only in the wee hours of the morning!

SHAKING HANDS

You can try teaching cats to "shake hands." Sometimes they will, but most of the time they seem to consider it beneath them, although it is obvious they realize what you expect.

LEASH TRAINING

Cats and kittens must have fresh air and sunshine. If you live in an apartment or house in the city where you can't let your cat run loose, leash training is important. If you have a female whom you don't want roaming the neighborhood "husband hunting," leash training is very important. The training, too, will prove a boon to you when you take your cat travelling by car.

It is rumored that Siamese cats are rather easily trained to walk on a leash. This is a myth. It is true that you often *see* leashed Siamese, but this is because people who have a valuable or distinctive cat hesitate to take the risks of letting him roam freely. They spend more time and patience training him, instead of just trying and giving up.

First, it is best to accustom the cat fully to the collar, by letting him sniff at it and perhaps bat it around a bit. Before you put it on him, pick him up and cuddle him, and assure him everything is fine. Show him you are not actually restricting his precious

Ballet Dancer Genze de Lappe and Dean Crane walk their pet Siamese cats in Central Park, New York City, every day. They realize that like dancers, cats need exercise to stay in trim. They also know how dangerous it is to take cats out without a leash. The leashes protect the cats from being struck down by a car, being chased by a dog, or being tormented by small children.

freedom, but enabling him to see more of the world. After he has become accustomed to the collar for a day or two, and can take it as a matter of course, then snap the leash on him (make sure it is lightweight) and let him walk around where he wants to go. When he finds he can still meander as he pleases, then gently start him going in the direction that *you* want. Most cats will fight the leash madly at the first authoritative tug. Your cat may "play dead" and not walk at all, being perfectly content to let you drag him around.

A cat that resists the leash in the house may change his mind if taken outdoors. It is, however, better to start the training inside as there is a minimum of distraction here, and your cat is on familiar ground.

If a kitten is trained young enough he won't mind a bit. Young kittens tend to learn fast.

A Siamese breeder in Ithaca, N. Y., has a queen that sits tied to the front porch and watches the cars go by. This cat also is content to be tied to a "trolley" run in the back yard (a wire strung from one tree to another, with the leash looped over it so the cat can run the length of the wire) for hours, with no danger of straying into other peoples' gardens or onto the road.

COMING WHEN CALLED

Any cat or kitten can easily be trained to come when you call "kitty, kitty." For some reason, it seems to be a natural and pleasing sound to them, so wherever they are, in or out, they come running. Start your cat on "kitty, kitty" when calling him to his meals. This is easier for him than responding to his name at first. After he gets to the age of understanding, then call "kitty" and his name, and gradually break him into coming to his name alone. If you start by calling his name, you will get the same result, although it may take a bit longer.

Did you call me? If cats don't have a better place, they will sometimes crawl into a small paper bag and make themselves comfortable.
When you call them, they will immediately awake from a sound
sleep, eyes wide open, looking for their master.

Unless your cat is trained to come when called, it is dangerous to have him running loose. Another cat may fight with him and you will be powerless to intercede unless you want a few scratches.

ROLLING OVER

Some cats can be trained to "roll over." Since a cat will roll over instinctively if you tickle his stomach, you can keep repeating "roll over" and tickling him when he does, until eventually he gets the idea. Cats like to be scratched, but when they, not you, desire it.

WORDS

Most cats catch on to individual words that you say, if you repeat them often enough. Cats soon come to understand "eat," "milk," "out," "bedtime," and similar short words. Words of one syllable are best. Repeat them always in the same tone of voice. Knowledge of words isn't actually considered a "trick," or even a "command," but it does make the relationship between your cats and you a bit more pleasant.

Your cats, if they do make word associations (for instance, associating "out" with going outdoors), will run to the door and

In training your cat, go just outside of the house with the cat on a long leash. You can let him go away from you and then pull on the leash as you call him to come.

mimic you. They are smart little things, but because of their independent natures, are too often underestimated.

TRICKS

Your cats' natural tricks and games (those they learn themselves, by copying what you do, or by sheer inventiveness) are just as good or better than what you can teach them to do. Kittens especially can keep you amused for hours, as they run and scamper, and pounce on imaginary mice. But cats hate to be laughed at! Laugh with them and they are happy, but laugh at them and they feel humiliated. You will immediately fall from their good graces.

Some cats are born showmen. They'll run and play around the house, but when visitors come in — the landlady, your cat-hating friend, or even the grocery boy — *then* they'll put on a show, running, jumping on the people, crying, being underfoot, or by remembering some of the tricks you have given up teaching.

Then there are the shy cats — you've taught them tricks and bragged about them. When friends drop in you can't even manage to find the beasts, and if you do they act as though you are totally insane and make it appear that this whole "trick" business is something you've just made up. Each cat is a personality in himself, and no two cats are alike.

My own cats have several self-taught tricks. Pandora takes the latch off the door when she wants to go out. All of my house cats have learned to sit on the window-sill by their feeding area when they feel a meal is in order. If they are outdoors and want to come in, they jump up and stare in the windows at me, following me from room to room.

Their favorite "trick" is turning the bedroom light off and on. (They are the light and power company's best customers!) Since this particular light is near the foot of the bed, for convenience I attached a cord to it so I could turn it off from the head of the bed. For hours (or until they are stopped) the cats, singularly or in groups, leap up and down, turning the light on and off. If I am reading in bed at night, they turn off the light when they feel it is time for me to retire.

You may not be too successful teaching them tricks, but they'll teach you in no time to understand and appreciate them.

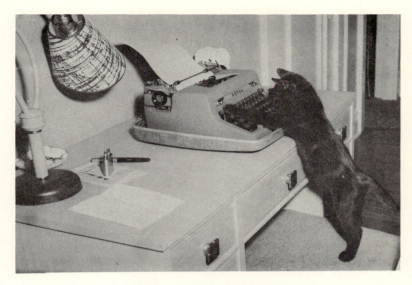

Cats can be taught tricks. The Black Domestic Short-hair (above) is
trying to type a letter asking for some catnip, while our piano virtuoso
(below) is a four-week-old tabby.

8. Health

Cats are healthy, hardy animals, but even as we, they get sick at times and meet with accidents. Never, *never* diagnose a disease yourself. Your veterinary went to college to learn this, so make use of his knowledge.

As soon as you acquire a kitten or cat, you should bring him to your veterinary for a medical check up. A little later your cat must have inoculations for feline enteritis, the most fatal and feared of any cat disease. If he has worms, and you can't get rid of them, the veterinary will.

If your cat never goes outside except on a leash, have his toenails clipped by the vet. This will save your furniture and your skin. If your cat goes out alone, don't have his claws clipped, as they are his main protection against enemies.

Don't clean your cat's ears. You will undoubtedly do more harm than good.

A cat does not mind heat and cold. He likes summer warmth and can also frolic in the snow with no difficulty. However, avoid drafts and sudden changes of temperature.

Vitamins are a "must" in a cat's diet. (This has been discussed in Chapter 4.)

Never give your cat patent medicines without the consent of your veterinary. Manufacturers sometimes recommend products that are unsafe, sometimes fatal for cats.

Lucky is the master whose cat likes to lap medicine from a spoon! Sometimes it is necessary to take your cat to a veterinary to get his medicine. If your cat will not lick it from the spoon he may take food that has the medicine in or on it.

GIVING MEDICINES

Giving medicine to a cat is more difficult than giving it to a dog. Your vet can show you the easiest way. Tasteless medicines may be mixed in with the food, or beaten up with milk. To give pills that cannot be ground up and mixed with food, take the cat *gently* by the scruff of the neck, pop the pill in his mouth, then blow on his nose. Hold his mouth closed until he has swallowed. Liquid medicine is best given with an eye dropper, preferably of hard rubber or polyethylene (soft) plastic. (If a cat chomps down on a glass eye dropper, the results may be disastrous.) Some cats accept medicine with no difficulty. Other cats may have to be wrapped up and held in a towel before they'll accept it. However, your cat will not disown you if you give him medicine — to him it's all part of the game.

FLEAS

Your most common problem will no doubt be fleas. Some cats who stay in the house all the time are lucky enough not to have

Start applying flea powder at the back of your cat's neck.

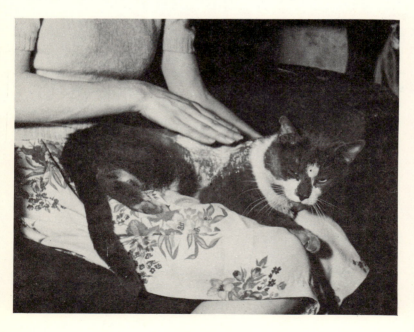

any, but most cats do. Do not buy a commercial flea powder unless your vet says it is all right for cats. The only safe product to kill cat fleas is rotenone (or derris powder). When you buy the rotenone powder, have your druggist mix it with ninety per cent plain, unscented and unmedicated talcum powder. This is cheap and very effective.

To apply the powder, start at the back of the cat's neck and sprinkle it well. Work it through the fur down to the skin, all over his head, chest, etc. Be extremely careful not to get any into his eyes, ears, nose and mouth. Then, go to the rear of the cat and do the same, starting with the back, where the tail begins. This keeps the fleas from retreating to either end, where cats are most sensitive. Then powder the back, sides and stomach, doing feet and tail last. Rub it all in well, and you'll be free of fleas for approximately two weeks.

RINGWORM

Cats rarely get ringworm, a disease that is hard to detect. The symptom is a rough spot on his coat, with the hair around it dry and breaking off, and the skin scabby. If you suspect your cat has ringworm, take him to your vet.

MITES

Mites are tiny little things. Ear mites, a quite common kind, revel in cats' ears, causing a dark discharge, reddened skin, itching and discomfort. This must be treated by a veterinary. Do not treat any ear disease at home, except under the instruction of a vet, as you may end up with a deaf cat or a dead one.

MANGE

Mange must be diagnosed and treated by a veterinarian. Symptoms are generally falling or rough and dry hair; scaly skin; little blisters; a scratching cat and discolored skin. Mange is caused by mange mites. It is communicable and spreads rapidly all over one cat, and then to others.

If you suspect your cat of having mange, isolate him until you can take him to your vet. Most veterinary hospitals won't keep a mangy cat, as the danger of communication is too great. Wash your hands after you touch him.

ECZEMA

Eczema looks similar to mange, but it is neither parasitic nor contagious. It stems from improper feeding, dirt and dampness. Your vet will diagnose it; pure olive oil will soothe it.

TICKS

Ticks are the most gruesome of the external parasites. They desensitize their victims and then dig their heads inside to suck the blood. Their bodies remain outside, swelling up with blood into large, reddish-brown blobs, which are easily recognized.

To get rid of these, drop alcohol on the imbedded tick. When it passes out, lift it off with tweezers and kill it by dropping it into a dish full of kerosene. Do not let any kerosene touch your cat, as it burns the skin.

WORMS

Worms are frequent in kittens, but not in all kittens. Do not treat worms yourself. Your veterinary will examine your cat's stool and determine what kind of worms (if any) he has, and will worm him accordingly. If your cat has worms, he may be sluggish, his coat will be dull, he will be thin but his stomach will protrude, and his breath will smell sickishly sweet. You may see worms in his feces or vomitus.

Roundworms, the most common, are long and round, and are generally expelled coiled. They are white and ugly. Tape-

If your cat has ticks, drop alcohol onto each red tick mark and await the tick's retreat from under the skin. When the tick comes out, pick it up with a pair of tweezers and kill it.

worms are excreted in small segments resembling small, brown rice grains. Your cat may drag his hind end along the floor to ease the itching and discomfort caused by the worms. He may eat more than usual; he may have alternating diarrhea and constipation.

VOMITING

If your cat throws his dinner up once, don't worry. It may have been the wrong temperature, or he may not have chewed it thoroughly. If he throws up more than once, watch closely for other symptoms. If you find hair or felt-like balls or strips in his vomitus, he has hair balls. If it is oddly colored, frothy, odoriferous, or bloody, bring him to your veterinary.

HAIR BALLS

Hair balls are the result of too little grooming. All the loose hairs cats lick off in their "baths" go into their stomachs where they pile up. Long-hair cats are more subject to this and need more grooming. The safe oils — vegetable oil, butter, or pure salad oil — will help him pass these. Never give your cat castor oil, as it is too strong. Mineral oil absorbs vitamins from food, and retards digestion. All oils should be given at room temperature. For a kitten, a teaspoonful is enough; a grown cat can use a tablespoonful.

CONSTIPATION

Constipation may be caused by hair balls. It may also be caused by improper feeding, insufficient exercise, or worms. Never give a cat a laxative other than the harmless oils mentioned above, or glycerine suppositories. If these do not work, take the cat to a vet. Never give a cat an enema.

FOREIGN OBJECTS

If your cat has something caught in his throat, he will cough and paw his throat and neck. Cover him with a large towel so he won't thrash around, then look in. Never try yourself to take bones or other foreign objects out of your cat's throat unless they are dull, unless you can see them at the top of his throat, and unless they have not broken the skin. If you do not see anything, or you see something sharp, rush him to your veterinary immediately!

If your cat has swallowed foreign matter, give him soft bulky

Long-hair cats, after constant licking of their coats, are more sus-ceptible to hair balls than short-haired cats. You can prevent this by constant brushing.

foods, such as bread soaked in meat juice, etc. Then, after he has eaten as much as he can, put a bit of salt on the back of his tongue to bring up the matter. If it doesn't come up, and you *know* he has swallowed something, watch him closely. If his stomach protrudes, if he vomits or has diarrhea, take him to the vet.

If your cat has swallowed string, do not attempt to pull up

the string. Cut it off at his mouth, give him lots of oil and wait. It should be passed within a few hours. If not, call the veterinary.

DIARRHEA

Diarrhea is generally caused by too much sloppy food. It is sometimes one symptom of worms. If firmer foods don't correct this condition, your vet will.

FELINE ENTERITIS

Feline enteritis, sometimes called cat distemper, is fast-moving, horrible and fatal. This is not the same disease as distemper in dogs. It is a disease of cats, and cats only. It can strike any cat anywhere, as germs are carried in the air, on the bottom of shoes, on hands, in any and all fashions. No cure will work unreservedly. An ounce of prevention is most assuredly worth a pound of cure!

The preventative is to have your cat inoculated when he is an eleven-week-old kitten. Two inoculations are given, ten days apart. They produce no after-effects, and then he will be safe the rest of his life. If a kitten younger than this is exposed, the vet can give him a temporary shot of serum which is effective for ten days.

A small kitten may die of the disease before he shows any signs of the illness. The general symptoms are fever, vomiting, diarrhea, runny eyes, poor coat and general malaise. The cat's legs spread out, and eventually he isn't able to stand up. A cat suspected of enteritis cannot be hospitalized, as the disease is too contagious.

If there is an epidemic in your area, have your vet give your inoculated cats booster shots, and your kittens temporary shots.

If you have had an infected cat, wait more than three months before bringing a new cat into the house. Burn all of the former cat's bedding, brushes, etc., and scrub your house thoroughly.

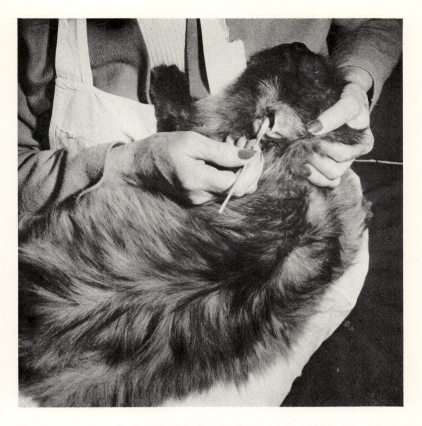

Examine your cat's ears regularly. If they need swabbing out do it carefully and watch out that you don't pierce the cat's ear if he moves suddenly.

FITS

Fits and convulsions occur most frequently in kittens, and are often caused by an overheated kitten eating cold food. Exhaustion and teething may also cause fits. If your cat has a fit, throw a towel over him, keep him quiet, and send for the vet. If the cat is conscious, give him only water. If the vet comes after the cat has "recovered," he should still examine him as he may be able to prevent a recurrence.

HEAT PROSTRATION

Heat prostration is most prevalent in old cats, overweight cats and very young kittens. Never play with a cat in the hot sun, or in very hot weather, unless the area is well shaded. Cats will avoid too much direct heat from the sun, if they can, and too much exercise in the heat. If your cat collapses, bring him indoors, gently massage him, and, if he is not unconscious, give him a drop of whiskey in water. *Call the veterinary.* Then, keep him quiet for a few days, and don't overfeed him. Give him more liquids, if possible.

RUNNING EYES

If your cat's eyes swell up and get red and runny, he may have conjunctivitis. Or he may have a cold, pneumonia or pneumonitis. Or it may be just a local irritation caused by a hair or speck of dirt.

The only safe treatment at home for a cat's or kitten's eyes is a bathing with a mild boric acid solution. Bathe the eyes frequently. If, in a day or two, you notice no change for the better, call your veterinary.

COLDS

When a cat has a cold, he must be kept warm and dry, and fed light but nourishing liquids. Give him a dose of olive oil to keep his bowels open. You may bathe his eyes with boric acid solution, and gently wipe his nose with a moist tissue. Feed him egg yolks and a little meat, along with increased liquids, to keep up his strength. If, in forty-eight hours you notice either no change, or a change for the worse, call your veterinary.

RABIES

Rabies in cats is rare, and needn't be worried about. If your cat is bitten by a rabid dog, wrap him up — or put him in a *closed* basket — and take him to your veterinary immediately.

A cat's eyes may begin running for a great many reasons. Bathe them with a mild boric acid solution for a few days, if they do not get better, you need professional advice from a veterinarian.

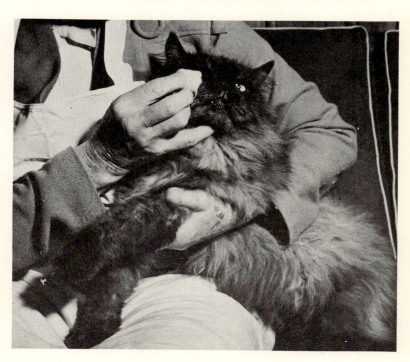

RESPIRATORY DISEASES

If your cat has chills, labored breathing or wheezing, fever (above 102.5° F.) or any weakness, take him to your veterinarian. He may have pneumonia, bronchitis, pneumonitis, or a similar disease. The veterinary will, if he sees fit, give him an antibiotic. Feed the cat eggnogs, raw beef, and a bit of oil, along with liquids.

POISON

If your cat has swallowed poison, or if you think he has, get a vet immediately! If you know what poison it was, tell the vet on the phone, and he will instruct you in proper first-aid measures. If the cat has been poisoned by household gas, rush him outside, call the vet, then use artificial respiration and try to revive him with spirits of ammonia or other smelling salts.

SNAKE BITE

If your cat should get bitten by a snake, call your veterinarian. Before he comes, administer snake bite serum as directed on the package, or slash the wound and suck out the blood and pour in whiskey. If the bite is on a leg, apply a tourniquet above the wound, releasing every ten minutes. Wash the wound in tepid running water for at least a half hour, if possible.

HEMORRHOIDS

Hemorrhoids are best treated by giving your cat a pure oil and rubbing the rectum with pure vaseline. Feed him softer foods for a day or two.

CUTS AND SCRATCHES

If your cat gets cut, whether by a knife, sharp edge, or the teeth of another animal, wash the cut well with soap and running

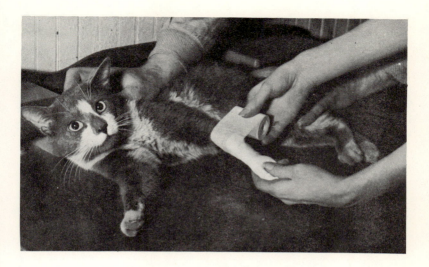

Only on rare occasions does a cat need first aid. If, however, your cat cuts himself on glass or is struck by a car, apply a tight bandage to stop the bleeding and get the cat to a veterinarian immediately.

water. Unless a vein or artery is slashed, let the wound bleed freely for a minute or two, to flush out some of the germs. If the cut is very deep, clip the fur around it. Wrap up the cut firmly with gauze soaked in boric acid solution.

If the cut is bleeding profusely, it is not necessary to wash it. The first thought in that case is to stop the flow of blood by stuffing gauze into the wound. If the cut is on a leg, then use a tourniquet between the cut and the cat's heart. Release the pressure on the tourniquet every ten minutes. Rush the cat to a veterinary.

A cat will lick slight scratches and clean and heal them better than your tender treatment, so leave these alone, unless there is a greenish or yellowish color to them, and an accumulation of pus.

This is a home-made collar to prevent a cat from scratching his head or ears.

BROKEN BONES AND FALLS

If your cat breaks a bone (tail bones are the most frequent) it should be set by a veterinarian immediately. If you suspect a broken bone, handle the cat as little and as gently as possible, and take him to your vet.

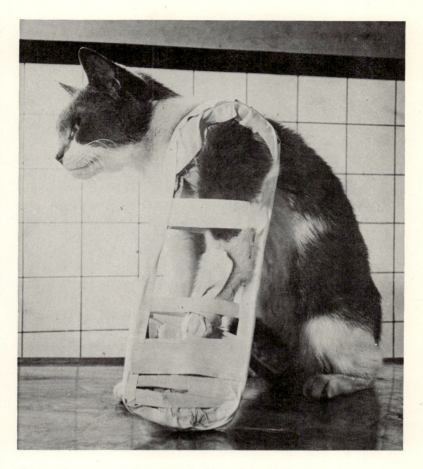

Ordinarily a cat with a broken leg is best disposed of, but he can learn to live like this for a while.

If the cat has fallen, but shows no symptoms of broken bones, it is possible that there may be internal injuries. In the case of a serious fall, don't feed him anything or fuss over him, for twenty-four hours. After this time, if he doesn't think he is "starving," call your vet. If he *is* hungry, give him eggnog and a small portion of raw beef. Watch his stool for blood; if he throws up or has trouble urinating, take him to your vet.

BURNS

Never use a patent medicine for a burn on a cat. If it is a slight burn, apply a saturated compress with a mild tea or baking soda solution to the affected part. If a large part of the cat got burned, cover all of the burned area with either olive oil or mineral oil, then take him to your veterinary. The same applies to scalds.

RICKETS

Your kitten should never be troubled by rickets. If he is, it is your fault, as improper feeding is the major cause of this crippling kitten disease. If your cat has short bowed front legs, enlarged joints, poor coat, bead-like lumps along the ribs, and a lack of energy, he probably has rickets. To prevent rickets and its accompanying malformations, kittens should have bone meal (*steamed* type only), cod liver oil and good food, plus fresh air and sunshine. Irradiated ergosterol, supplementary calcium and vitamins may also be needed. Your veterinary will be able to tell you what your own cat needs most.

TEETH

Kittens chew and gnaw when they are teething. They also chew and gnaw for the fun of it. Your kitten should have no trouble shedding his milk teeth for firm adult, meat-eater teeth. If a tooth is loose, and is causing the cat trouble, you can pull it out carefully with tweezers. Cats swallow their teeth — it's perfectly normal.

Older cats, and very old cats, sometimes have toothaches, as

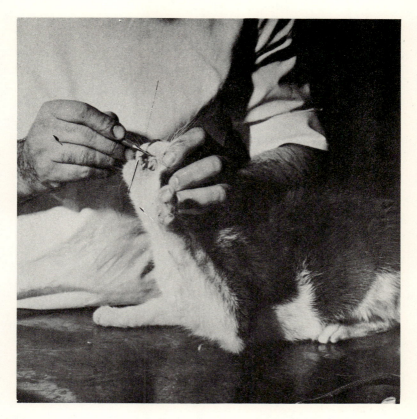

Examine your cat's teeth from time to time and remove the tartar or foreign debris that sticks close to the gums. Usually a cat's teeth will remain perfect throughout his life if he is fed a well-balanced diet.

their teeth decay with time. If your cat doesn't eat well, has trouble chewing, or continually paws his face and shakes his head, look inside his mouth. If there is discoloration of the gums or signs of abcesses, take him to the vet, where the offending member will be extracted and the abscess healed. Bad breath often accompanies tooth and mouth disorders.

THE SICK CAT

Whenever your cat is sick, keep him away from bright lights. Yet, do not let him go off into a corner by himself. A cat will talk himself into dying if he feels he is not loved enough, or if he is permitted to go away and sulk. Keep him eating, if possible, even if it is only a bit of milk and broth, or whatever your veterinary prescribes.

Handling a sick cat is bad. When he wants attention, he will come to you and sit on your lap. If he is too weak, lift him up, *gently,* and then leave him alone except to stroke him, if he wishes.

When a cat doesn't feel well, do not bathe him, no matter how dirty he gets. Avoid (at any time) the use of cloths impregnated with "cleaner" that are said to "dry clean" cats. Many of these are for dogs only, and have chemicals and flea repellants in them that will poison your cat, or irritate his skin. Also, most cats will not tolerate the smell. As a sick cat won't bathe himself, it is important to continue with your cat's daily grooming, to keep his coat in good condition.

Never give your cat any commercial product for illnesses or for cleanliness that your veterinary hasn't first approved.

Never use DDT in your house or let your cat near it.

Do not pet other cats if your cat is ill, and never pet ill cats belonging to other people.

To prevent strangulation, always make sure a cat's head is straight and not tilted back when giving him medicine.

9. The Cat's World

Cats are naturally curious, and like to explore new places and things. Their curiosity is often their undoing . . . "Curiosity killed a cat. . . ." The last part of this adage, ". . . satisfaction brought him back," is not necessarily true. Cats are, however, very quick at catching on. Once they have invesigated a hot stove or a cigarette, all stoves and all cigarettes are taboo.

Because of their curiosity, cats are what we term "destructive." They are also destructive because of other instincts: the instinct to scratch and flex their claws; to pounce on moving objects, then shred them; to get their food by theft. They are destructive from sheer playfulness. To minimize torn furniture, a scratching post should be made or bought and every time the cat scratches the furniture, he should be brought to it (see Chapter 6).

Toys and an old sock or rag doll of his very own will satisfy most of your cat's chewing and gnawing, and will keep him away from your better things. If you give a cat an old sock to chew, he won't (contrary to some opinions) think he may chew *all* socks. His "pride of possession" will satisfy him.

TRAVELING AND SHIPPING

Cats are great travelers. All but a very few like to travel by car. Those who don't are generally older cats who have never done it before.

When traveling in the car, be sure that your cat is leashed,

A cat carrier, such as this, is needed when taking your cat long distances on a public conveyance. This type of plastic enclosed case eliminates drafts and is pleasant for the cat, but it invites nosy stares.

and that no windows are open wide enough for him to jump through. Also, be careful that he doesn't annoy the driver. When driving alone with your cat or cats, it is best to put him or them in a cat carrier.

The cat carrier, which is relatively inexpensive, makes it much easier at all times to transport even one cat, especially if you would otherwise have to carry him in your arms. You can instead buy a wicker basket, with a lid — the weave lets in air. Most cats do not mind this form of travel. Koki (a Siamese of mine) used to run and sit by her leash when she wanted to go out; after she had ridden in the carrier a couple of times, she would run and sit by that, or, if the lid was up, jump in!

When traveling by rail, a cat carrier is a necessity. It is better to have your cat with you than to check him in the baggage car, where he will be subjected to drafts and frightening noises. Some cats will go out cheerfully in boats . . . Booty-Too, a Domestic Short-hair, loved rowboats. Most cats like planes too.

A harness is a bit better than a collar for walking a cat, and for car travel the harness is ninety-nine per cent better. If the cat should slip, or take a tumble, you know he won't break his neck.

When shipping cats, crate them well, mark the crate with the contents, and insure for the cat's value (or more). Ship *only* by Air Express, and never around the holiday season. Either you or someone else should be waiting at the other end for the cat's arrival.

Since cats are relatively little trouble when traveling by car, and since they are acceptable in all the better motels, it is better to bring your cat with you, if possible, than to leave him behind with a friend or at a boarding kennel. Cats are of great comfort after a long day's drive — new antics to match new places will refresh you immeasurably. Feeding en route is no problem — most cats will eat on the floor of the car, from their dish, and most restaurants accept them, especially in a carrier. Your cat's pan can be put on the floor in the back of the car, and in no time he'll learn to use it when the car is in motion. He'll pick any- where to sleep — my cats usually sleep on the rear window deck, or in the crown of my husband's hat!

In going into a motel, bring in the cat and his pan first, put them in the bathroom, and shut the door. Check first to make sure he can't get out of the window. This will keep him from running out of the door or from getting underfoot while you bring in your luggage. After you've gotten all the doors closed for the final time, let him out of the bathroom to explore for a few minutes, then feed him. He'll quickly make himself at home.

CATS AND DOGS

If you already have a dog, it is perfectly fine and safe to bring in your new cat or kitten. First, however, make sure the cat's claws have been blunted. Do not come rushing in and present Fido with his new playmate; but do not hide them from each other. Try not to give Fido any less attention, although that will be hard to do.

A kitten should adjust faster to the dog, and a young dog will adjust better to a cat than an old one. Getting a puppy and a kitten at the same time works out well, as they are both young, and so busy getting acquainted with their new surroundings that they haven't time to fight! Most dogs will learn very quickly to respect a cat, and in no time they will be fast friends. As soon as you see them eating from the same dish, and sleeping together, you can relax.

Cats and dogs have a fine sense of ownership and priority. To illustrate, there were once two cats, Blackie and Lex, and two dogs, Tom and Sam. Tom and Sam lived in the left hand half of a duplex house, with the cats in the other. This house had a common porch, with two sets of stairs leading up from the ground, a set on either side of the middle. Blackie, Lex, Tom and Sam took their walks together, and hunted, visited and played together. But when it was time to go home every night they would separate at the bottom of the porch, the dogs going up their steps, and Blackie and Lex up theirs. And, when they slept or sunned themselves on the porch, none of them would cross the invisible center line, even to play. They would all solemnly walk down their own steps, and *then* meet for recreation.

Cats and dogs cooperate, too. One example of this was Beta, a Manx. Beta lived in an apartment, near some woods. Except

A cat and a dog can learn to get along together. It's easier if they are both young, but can work out if you are careful in introducing them when they are both mature.

for a large English bulldog, he was the only animal in the area, he thought. So, Beta and the dog became acquaintances. Then one day as Beta was out sunning himself, a large black cat appeared from the woods and began chasing him, round and round the building. Beta couldn't get away, nor did he dare stop running. Suddenly he spied his friend the bulldog, sunning himself. Beta ran up behind the sleeping dog, and waited for the interloper to catch up. Sure enough, round the corner of the apartment came the black cat, with fire in his eye, intent on getting Beta. But, he came to a sudden halt — he had seen the dog!

Here are a Great Dane and a Siamese who have been raised together from their first month of life. They even eat from the same dish . . . the dog eats cat food and the cat likes dog food.

CATS AND OTHER CATS

Cats and cats, and kittens and cats (other than direct offspring), adjust differently and more vocally than dogs and cats. Oddly enough, it is generally the newcomer who raises the most ruckus. He is scared, and has *so* many things on his mind, that he seems to jump at his own shadow. The already-situated cat is on common ground, and generally not frightened, only protective of what is his. Very frequently the older cat who "belongs" will object to the new one's use of his eating and sleeping areas, pan, and even your lap.

This dog and cat team actually sleeps together (though they do not stay under the covers for very long!). They are such close friends, they will fight each other's enemies.

A kitten seems to adjust in a couple of days, a grown cat in a week or two. Never force the cats together; give them separate dishes (of course, each will think the other's better and exchange); pick them up separately, etc. As with dogs, give the first-owned more attention than usual. The new cat will be too excited to have it do him much good, and your older cat will need it. By this, I don't mean to ignore the little stranger . . . you love him and no doubt he is too cute to resist. But do try to be fair. After the cats have eaten and slept together peaceably, all is well. They are a team now, and devoted to each other. They will band together to run out other "unwanted guests."

Two of my cats, Koki and Pan, have found a new way of attacking intruders. Often the intruding cat will run under a low object and hide, where he is "safe." Koki runs in front of the skulking cat, luring him out, and Pan, the fighter, chases him away.

When we first brought home one of our studs, Phra Shri Yhu Tu (Siamese) the other cats didn't know what to make of him. They were friendly at first, until his growl and hiss (the biggest parts of him, as he was a "wee kit") made them wary. Then, he settled down and, after several days, they forgot his ill manners and accepted him socially. After a few weeks, he became their "baby" — they fought for him, and washed him, for all the world like little girls with a new doll.

It is amazing what games cats will play together. Like children, they compete in jumping, racing, climbing, and other games of skill. They also play tag, follow-the-leader, hide and go seek, and other obviously "fun" games.

If a guest comes to your house with a cat, it is best to ignore all of the cats. They'll growl and usually both sides will declare a truce and hide. Many times if you have feline visitors who use the toilet-pan, your cat may run in and dig out all the sand after the guest has left. Then, he won't "go" until it is refilled.

HAVING KITTENS

Most cats have no difficulty delivering kittens. It is a natural thing, and should be treated as such. However, there are a few pointers to keep in mind.

If possible, before she is bred, have her checked by a veterinary. If she is a small cat, or has had a case of rickets, she may not be able to deliver the kittens properly. Also, have her checked at least once during her pregnancy. At about the fifth week of pregnancy, give the prospective mother more food. Give her (especially) milk — as much as she'll drink — and beef and eggs Give her pure salad or olive oil as a preventative for constipation

Getting a cat to accept a parakeet as a pal is quite an accomplishment, to say the least. This team actually eats and sleeps together.

every second or third day. She should have exercise, but not strenuous leaping or jumping.

A cat carries her kittens 63 days. In a young queen they may be born about the 58th or 60th day; in an old cat perhaps up to the 64th or 65th day. A veterinary is generally not needed, but it is wise to have one on call, especially if it is the cat's (and your) first experience. If her time goes past 65 days, call the vet. If the queen is in labor for more than four hours, or is bleeding excessively, or is having difficulties expelling the kittens, or seems really *sick*, call your vet immediately.

The kittens are expelled in a membrane sack, which the mother cat normally eats. Generally it will be only one kitten if it is the first time, but later litters will contain as many as six or eight. After the kits are born, leave them alone with the

Cats have a natural desire to catch and eat fish and mice. Only a well-trained cat will pose for a picture like this.

mother cat when you have ascertained: that they will not be squashed or smothered; that they are in a dimly-lit place, small enough so the kittens cannot become misplaced; and that the cat has enough milk to feed them with. The latter is assured by gently pressing Mama's teats between forefinger and thumb. If a drop of milk shows, all is well. Most cats are well prepared by nature for this, but if there is no milk appearing within six hours, call your veterinary.

If there are too many kittens, or if any kitten is dead or deformed, take away the unwanted ones immediately. Have your veterinary or the ASPCA put them away quickly and painlessly. If the kits are left with their mother before they are destroyed, she will later miss them. Leave at least one kitten for her. Do not remove all the cat's kittens, unless it is absolutely necessary — if they are all born dead, or if the mother cat is too ill for them (to be decided only by a veterinarian). In this event it will be necessary for you to massage the milk out of the mother cat's nipples frequently. Your veterinary will tell you how often to do this, and show you how.

As the queen nurses her young, she should get the same food as when pregnant. After approximately three weeks, you may start decreasing the number of feedings, and increasing the rations, so at six to eight weeks after the kittens have been born the cat is back to normal, but still vitaminized, feedings. From there on, Mama will train and wean the kits by herself, with a little help from you. When the kittens are three weeks old, you may begin feeding them a little scraped raw beef (see Chapter 4).

CAT CONVERSATIONS

Now for a bit about how your cat converses. He talks to other cats by his facial expressions, some of them too delicate for us to even notice. He talks to them with his eyes, whiskers, and body. His "meow" is primarily for conveying messages to people, who just can't seem to understand him otherwise.

Some of the more obvious signs cats use are:
Fluffed up tail — fright
Tail drooping — disgust or fatigue, possible ill health
Lashing tail — anger or annoyance
Tail in the air — gay, good health
Growl — anger
Purr — contentment
A light, upwardly inflected "meow" — a question. When addressed to another cat, usually means "Come play."
Ears flattened against head — intense anger
Ears tilted backward — displeasure
Ears pricked far forward — attention
Whiskers forward — curiosity
Rubbing of whiskers on you or an object — love or desire
Fur ruffled up — too cold, or ill health

Your cat's ears also act as miniature radar units, turning toward sounds.

After a cat returns from outdoors, and his feline companion has remained in, the first thing he'll do is hunt up his little buddy, and touch noses. This reassures him that all is well and as it should be.

If you have had more than one cat, and your numbers are decreased because of necessity or death, for several days the cat who remains will hunt through the house, mewing and crying, looking for his friend. Another cat won't take the old one's place — your cat may just induce the newcomer to help look for the "lost" cat!

You will soon grow accustomed to the actions of your own cat, and know what they mean — as he will cope with yours — and your happiness together will thrive.

10. How to Show Your Cat

Any cat at all can be shown! This will surprise you if you thought that only the "aristo-cats" of felinity were eligible. For shows, The American Cat Association, Inc. has over 350 classes, and the Cat Fanciers' Association, Inc. over 500! The United Cat Federation, Inc., The Cat Fanciers Federation, and the American Cat Fanciers Association also have about as many classes, so you see, there is room for one and all and especially for your pet.

THE "DANGERS" OF SHOWING

The dangers of showing are often discussed. Non-showers are forever harping on the dangers of showing. Granted, there is a risk — but the great pleasures and thrills you get are experiences which more than compensate for the minor everyday hazards.

Disease is the first danger that comes to mind. How valid is the danger? No one is permitted to show a cat that has had a contagious disease, or that has had contact with a diseased cat within the past 21 days. This allows full time for latent diseases to show themselves. A breeder shouldn't show a sick cat — since a sick cat is never at its best. (All the clubs have stiff penalties against members showing diseased animals.) There is a veterinarian at every cat show. He checks each entry, disqualifying any cats showing symptoms of disease. The show cages are all thoroughly cleaned before they are used; the vet, the judges, and

The author points out some of the ribbons and diplomas she has won recently. Cat shows, which bring people together for a common purpose, add to the fun of keeping cats.

stewards wash their hands before handling any cat; the judging cages are disinfected after each use.

As for the mental dangers of a show for your cat, most cats and kittens are unaffected. To be sure, a house cat may not like a cage, but your love and the cat's natural curiosity help him to take it in his stride. A very shy cat may strenuously object to being shown in a cage, but the cages are roomy and most cats are either born showmen or simply sleep through the whole show!

The advantages of shows are many: they help to uphold the various breeds' standards; they enable you to compare your cats with the very best in catdom; you can get an honest evaluation of your cat . . . whether you should use him for breeding or not (if you have a pure-bred) . . . how he stands up with the others;

you meet similarly-minded folk, and have a chance to discuss cats and related problems to your heart's content — and last but not least, the ribbons! Nothing is quite as much of an ego-booster as a pretty rosette, or a silky ribbon, and the pride of ownership that accompanies it!

So you have decided to show! Wonderful! Now your major problem is to find a show!

HOW TO FIND A SHOW

Any of the five major associations (see page 28) will gladly tell you of an affiliated club in your area; shows are advertised in the newspapers; many of the magazines carry the notices; *All-Pets* magazine and *Cats* magazine publish the show listings every month; a breeder in the area will help you; even some pet stores have show information.

When you have located a show, write to the club secretary, and request a copy of show rules of the sponsoring organization, entry blanks, and the "specials" (closing date for entries, list of classes, fees, time, etc.). Generally the closing date for entries is approximately a month from the time of the show, although it may vary.

The fees are usually very reasonable, ranging between $1.00 and $3.00 per cat, depending upon the size of the show; whether you are entering in All Breed class only (or Specialty plus All Breed) and whether the cat is registered with the sponsoring organization. If the cat is not registered, a *listing fee* to list your cat with the show manager must be paid. This usually is 50¢; very often house pets, neuters and spays are excepted from this listing.

ENTRY BLANKS

On the entry blank you will be asked to fill in the following information: Breed — if your household pet is not an "accepted" breed, then fill in "Domestic Short-hair"; color; sex; eye color;

registration number, or listing; name; birthday; breeder (if owner of your cat's mother is not known to you, just write "unknown"); sire and dam (either their names, or "unknown"); agent (if you are shipping your cat, or sending him with someone else); your name and address; the class numbers of specialty class and all breed competitions, and what specialty class, if any, your cat is to be entered in.

Cats may be exhibited only, or entered in competition for sale. To be sold at the show, any cat or kitten over 4 months old (generally) *must* be entered in competition.

After you have returned the entry blank and the fee to the show manager, you will be sent an acknowledgment. Save this, as some shows require it at show time!

GETTING INTO "SHOW SHAPE"

Getting your cat in "show shape" is the next hurdle. Presumably, he should be in good condition already, but if not, here are some tips.

Groom your cat every day. Once a week, groom with a rubber curry comb, as used on horses. Use your hands to polish him. If your cat is a Long-hair, gently comb him, and remove all the mats from his fur. Feed him a diet supplement for internal help: cod liver oil, or one of the "fats" that your vet can recommend. If the coat is very poor, use *pure* lanolin, obtainable from a pharmacist at about half the price of prepared lanolin creams. Rub it into the skin and fur every other day. Groom often with that soft brush, for a real shine.

THE SHOW CAGE

To show a cat to the public to his best advantage, most of the show people use drapes and decorations in the cages. (Check with the show manager first, however, for the judging must be done in a separate area — it usually is — or else decorating is forbidden.) You may decorate the cage any way you wish, as

Get your cat into "show shape" before you take her to the show. This includes daily grooming for weeks before the show, and addition of vitamin supplements to the diet. Don't bring in an unkempt cat.

long as you keep it all on the inside! If you make drapes, make them the full width of the material, as cages vary in height (although most are 24" x 24" in length and width). You may want to put a pillow on the cage floor for your cat to sleep on. Do bring your cat's own pan and his own "sanitary material," paper, litter or dirt. Sawdust is not allowed because of the fire

Often the man must accept cats because his wife loves them. Sometimes men who were reluctant to have cats in the house, become show enthusiasts.

hazard. Many shows supply litter, but to be sure, bring your own. Also bring dishes for food and water, and a small amount of your cat's favorite food.

You may also like to have alcohol, to wash your hands and the cage; scotch tape; grooming equipment (a must); a clear plastic to cover the front of the cage so that people won't put their fingers in; safety pins; Q-tips; cotton. All are helpful! You really can't determine individual needs until you get there.

Bring along a certificate from your vet certifying that your cat has had his inoculations for enteritis. *A cat must be inoculated in order to be shown,* but not all veterinaries provide proof. However, it is better to be safe than sorry!

At the show, no cat will be allowed in the cage until he has been checked by a vet. Therefore, arrive perhaps a half an hour early, so you can find your number, and fix up the cage. When the vet arrives, the cats and owners will line up, and each will be checked in turn. After your cat is "passed," he can be put in his cage. Comfort him a while, then make use of your time to view your competition, and meet new friends.

THE JUDGING

Then to the judging! When your class is called, a show steward will take your cat from his cage, and carry him to the judging cages. The purpose of this is to insure fair judging — a judging of cat and not owner. At a very small informal show, you may be asked to escort your cat to the judge yourself. Don't worry about the stewards and your cat; they are responsible cat lovers, who have had years of experience handling cats. In a very big class, only a few cats are called up at a time, the poorer ones being sent back.

The judge will pick up your cat and examine him closely. She'll look at his coloring, his body and tail, his general proportions and conformation, his head and ears, his eyes, his coat and his condition. The *housepet class,* which you may be entered in, is judged solely on beauty and condition. The judge may look at your cat once or she may look several times. Your cat may stay in the judging cage a while, or he may be returned immediately. If he is returned, don't feel badly. He isn't the only one! Your competition has been returned before, too. Generally, as you compare, you can see your own animal's good and bad points, but if you have questions, the judges will be glad to talk with you, after all the judging has been completed.

Your pet will be called up again, for the "all breed." Two judges evaluate the cat in this event. Your cat may take a ribbon in this class and not in the other.

The golden rule in cat showing: Never be a poor loser. Congratulate the winners, as you would like to have been congratulated. If the judge feels it is worth your while, try again at another show.

Perhaps you would have been better entering in a larger show . . . or a smaller one. Don't give up on the first try, unless a judge (and judges' opinions vary too!) advises you to get better stock. Remember, your household pet class observes no standards other than beauty and condition! One judge's idea may differ radically from that of another!

No one may leave the show unless granted special permission, until after the judging is over.

When you get your cat home, watch him for a week or two. If he gets running eyes, diarrhea, or you notice some other condition that is not normal, call your veterinarian. Tell him the cat has been shown and be prompt in reporting any "symptoms." If your cat has picked up a bug, the vet will be able to cure him before he is ill! Generally you won't have to worry, as all possible precautions are taken.

STANDARDS OF THE CAT FANCIERS' ASSOCIATION, INC.

Judges' Score

To be applied to all Breeds and Colors except Siamese, Manx, Abyssinian, Russian Blue and Burmese.

Color	25
Coat	15
Condition	10
Head (including size and shape of eyes)	20
Type (including shape, size, bone and length of tail)	20
Color of eyes	10
Total	100

In all tabby varieties the 25 points allowed for color to be divided 15 for markings and 10 for color.

LONG-HAIR STANDARD

TYPE: The perfect cat should be of cobby type, that is to say, low on the legs, deep in the chest, massive across the shoulders and rump, with a short well-rounded middle piece. In size the cat should be large or medium, but there should be no sacrifice of quality for the sake of mere size.

HEAD: The head should be round and massive, with great breadth of skull, and be well set on a neck not too long. EARS: Neat, round tipped, set far apart and not unduly open at the base. NOSE: Short, snub and broad. CHEEKS: Full. JAWS: Broad and powerful.

EYES: Large, round, full, set far apart and brilliant, giving a sweet expression to the face.

TAIL: Short, carried without a curve and at angle lower than the back, but not trailed, when walking.

BACK: Level.

LEGS: Thick and strong; forelegs perfectly straight.

PAWS: Large, round and firm,—toes carried close; five in front and four behind.

COAT: Long hair. The coat should show primarily perfect physical condition. It should be of fine texture, soft, glossy, full of life and should stand off from the body. It should be long all over the body, including the shoulders. The ruff should be immense and continue in a deep frill between the front legs. Ear tufts, long, curved. Toe tufts, long. Brush very full.

UNDESIRABLE: Rangy, flat-sided, narrow-chested, long, spindle-legged, long-tailed cats, with long noses, large ears, pointed and upright, eyes set bias or close together, receding chins, light bone and a general "foxy" face.

WHITE: Pure white, no colored hairs. Eyes, deep blue or deep orange.

BLACK: Dense coal black, sound from roots to tip of fur; absolutely free from any tinge of rust on tips or smoke in undercoat. Eyes, copper or deep orange.

BLUE: Color blue not drab, lighter shade preferred, one level tone, without shading or marking from nose to tip of tail, and sound to the roots. Eyes, brilliant copper or deep orange.

RED: Deep, rich, clear, brilliant red without shading, markings, or ticking; lips and chin same color as coat. Eyes, brilliant copper or deep orange.

CREAM: One level shade of cream, sound to the roots. Eyes, brilliant copper or deep orange.

CHINCHILLA: The undercoat should be pure white, the coat on back, flanks, head and tail being sufficiently tipped with black to give the characteristic sparkling silver appearance; the legs may be very slightly shaded with the tipping, but chin, ear tufts, stomach and chest must be pure white; any barring or brown or cream tinge is a fault. Eyes to be green. Rims of eyes, lips and nose to be outlined with black. Center of nose to be brick red.

SHADED SILVER: Shaded Silver should be pure, unmarked silver, shading gradually down the sides, face and tail, from dark on the ridge, to white on chin, chest and belly and under the tail; the legs to be the same tone as the face. The general effect to be much darker than a Chinchilla. Any barring or brown or cream tinge to be considered a fault. Eyes to be green. Rims of eyes, lips and nose to be outlined with black. Center of nose to be brick red.

SMOKE: A Smoke cat should appear black, with white undercoat and black points and mask, light silver frill and ear tufts. Eyes to be brilliant copper or deep orange.

SILVER TABBY: Color should be a pale clear silver with broad, dense black markings; to conform in pattern to those described for Brown Tabby; any brown or cream tinge to be considered a fault; eye color, green or hazel preferable. Orange eyes acceptable.

BROWN TABBY: Ground color, including lips and chin, rich and tawny. Markings dense black, clearly defined and broad (not narrow pencilings). Legs, evenly barred, the "bracelets" coming up high to meet the body markings. Tail barred. Barring on neck and chest, or "necklaces" distinct, like so many chains. Head barred. Cheek swirls and swirls on sides of body, each continuing in an unbroken ring. The marks upon the face and between the ears and down the neck to meet the "butterfly" on the shoulders, which divides the head lines from the spine line. Back markings, to consist of a distinct black stripe down the middle of the back with stripes of the ground color on either side of it, and black lines on either side of them. No ticking. Eyes, copper or deep orange; copper preferred.

RED TABBY: Ground color, red, markings (as described for Brown Tabby) to be a deep rich red. No ticking. Eyes, copper or deep orange.

TORTOISE-SHELL: Black, orange, and cream, bright, clearly defined and well-broken even to the feet. Patched, not brindled. Desirable, half of nose black, half orange, known as the "blaze". No tabby markings. Eyes, copper or deep orange.

CALICO: (Tortoise-shell and White): Three colors, black, red, and cream to be well distributed, clearly patched, and interspersed with white. White should be in distinct, predominant areas on chest, face, legs, and paws. White blaze is desirable. Eyes, brilliant deep orange or copper. Faults: Blending of colors; brindling; white hairs in colored patches. Tabby markings to be penalized. Black feet undesirable.

BLUE CREAM: The two colors, blue and cream, well-divided and broken into patches; bright and well-defined. No ticking. Eyes, brilliant copper or deep orange.

OBJECTIONS IN TORTOISE-SHELL AND BLUE CREAM: Colors brindled rather than broken, solid color on face, legs or tail.

DOMESTIC SHORT-HAIR STANDARD

BODY AND TAIL: Well knit and powerful, showing good depth of body. Chest full and broad. Tail short rather than long, tapering towards point, carried almost level with back.

LEGS AND FEET: Legs of good substance and in proportion to the body. Feet neat and well rounded.

HEAD: Broad between the ears; cheeks well developed; face and nose short.

EARS: Small, slightly round at tips, not large at base.

COAT: Short, smooth and very close lying.

CONDITION: Hard and muscular, giving a general appearance of activity.

COLOR: Requirements for color of coat and eye color the same as for long-haired cats.

FAULTS: Too high on legs; receding chin.

SIAMESE STANDARD

SEAL POINT

Scale

BODY COLOR _____ 15

Even pale fawn or cream, shading gradually into a lighter color on the stomach and chest. The coat color should not be gray. In judging body color in older cats, allowance should be made for darker coats as Siamese generally darken with age but there should be definite contrast between body color and points. Kittens, lighter in color. Point allotment; Proper color, 4 points; Proper shading, 4; Evenness of color, 7.

POINTS _____ 10

Mask, ears, legs, feet, and tail, dense and clearly defined, all of the same shade of deep seal brown. Mask should be connected by tracings with the ears, except in kittens. Point allotment: Mask, 2; Ears, 2; Legs, 2; Feet, 2; Tail, 2.

BODY TYPE _____ 20

The body should be medium in size, dainty, long and svelt. Males to be proportionately larger than females. Neck, long and slender. Legs, proportionally slim; hind legs slightly higher than the front. Feet, small and oval in shape. Tail, long and tapering with no visible kinks. Point allotment: Body, 7; Neck, 4; Legs and feet, 5; Tail, 4.

HEAD _____ 20

Head should be long and should taper in straight lines from the ears to a narrow muzzle, with no break at the whiskers. The receding chin caused by the failure of the upper and lower teeth to meet in a straight line shall be considered a serious fault. The skull is to be flat, and the nose is to be a continuation of the forehead with no break. In profile, a straight line is to be seen from the center of the forehead to the tip of the nose. Allowance is to be made for jowls in the stud cat. There should be the width of an eye between the eyes. Ears rather large and pricked, wide at the base. Allotment of points: Long flat profile, 6; Fine muzzle, 4; Non-receding chin, 4; Width between eyes, 2; Ears, 4.

EYES—COLOR AND SHAPE _____ 20

Eyes shall be clear and of a vivid deep blue color. Eye aperture almond in shape and slanting towards the nose in true Oriental fashion. Point allotment: Color, 10; clear, 5; deep blue, 5; shape, 10; Oriental, 5; uncrossed, 5.

COAT _____ 10

Short, fine in texture, glossy, and lying close to the body. Allotment of points: Short coat, 3; Fine coat, 2; Glossy coat, 2; Close coat, 3.

CONDITION _____ 5

Good physical condition. Not fat; inclined to muscle.

BLUE POINT

The above standard is to apply to the Blue Point Siamese except that the coat is to be bluish white, changing gradually to an oyster white on stomach and chest. Points to be of a much darker blue, but of the same tone as the coat. There must be no fawn in the coat. Kittens, lighter in color. Eyes, China blue.

CHOCOLATE POINT

The Seal Point standard applies to the Chocolate Point Siamese with the following exceptions: Points; milk chocolate color, the ears, mask, legs, feet, and tail to be even in color. The ears should not be darker than the other points. Eyes, clear, bright China blue. Pale or slatey eyes are to be discouraged. Body, ivory color all over. Gray or dingy shading to be a fault. Foot pads, cinnamon pink.

FROST POINT (TEMPORARY STANDARD)   *Scale*

BODY COLOR ⸺⸺⸺⸺⸺⸺⸺⸺⸺⸺⸺ 15

Even glacial white without shading.

POINTS ⸺⸺⸺⸺⸺⸺⸺⸺⸺⸺⸺⸺⸺ 10

Frost gray of pinkish tone. In the mature cat, the mask, legs, feet, and the outer surface of the ears to be as even in color as possible. The mask to be complete and to be connected by tracings with the ears.

SHAPE—BODY AND TAIL ⸺⸺⸺⸺⸺⸺⸺ 20

Same as for the Seal Point, but generally smaller in size. The Frost Point matures when between two and three years of age. The cat must not be penalized for size if it is well proportioned and of good comformation.

HEAD AND EARS ⸺⸺⸺⸺⸺⸺⸺⸺⸺ 20

Same as for Seal Points. Inner surface of the

ears, a delicate peach blossom tone. Nose leather,
a faded lilac hue at the tip.

EYES 20

Shape and slant as for Seal Points. Color, clear
China blue. Pale or slatey eyes discouraged.

COAT AND CONDITION 15

Same as for Seal Points.

Note: Color of foot pads in Frost Points, salmon pink.

UNDESIRABLE FOR ALL SIAMESE

Round-headed, fat, thick-set specimens. Hood (A continuation or an extension of the point coloring over the
top of the head, around the sides and under the throat.
The mask instead of fading away gradually at throat,
makes a distinct change in color so it would appear that
a hood was tied around the head. Tracings to the ears are
lost as the mask continues up between the ears.) Rough
or shaggy coats. Odd eye color; gray or yellowish tinge
in eyes; crossed eyes. Belly and hip spots. Tabby or ticked
markings. Light hairs in points. White feet or toes. Receding chin. Gray coat in Seal Points. Fawn coat in Blue Points.

ABYSSINIAN STANDARD

COLOR AND TICKING 35

Color—Ruddy brown, ticked with various shades
of darker brown or black. Inside of belly and forelegs should be of a tint to harmonize with the main
color, preference being given to orange brown.
Ears and tail tipped with dark brown or black.
Nose, tile red. Paw pads black, this color to extend
up back of hind legs to the first joint. Ticking—two
or more bands of color on each hair—to count 10
points.

TYPE—BODY AND TAIL 25

Body—rather long, lithe, and graceful, showing

well-developed muscular strength. Legs proportionally slim. Feet neat, round, and compact. Tail thick at base, fairly long and tapering. The distinctive Abyssinian conformation strikes a medium between cobbiness and the extremely svelt and lengthy type.

HEAD AND EARS 15

Head should be triangular but not sharply pointed at the chin. Ears large, pointed, and well set, broad at the base.

EYES 10

Almond shaped, brilliant, and expressive. Color— gold, green, or hazel. The more depth and richness in color, the better.

COAT 10

Soft and silky, dense, fine in texture.

CONDITION 5

UNDESIRABLE

White anywhere. *Bars, rings, and other tabby markings are serious faults and should be penalized.* Coldness (grayish tone) in color. Cobby body. Scanty tail. Short, heavy legs or spayed feet. Round head. Small ears. Pale eyes. Coarse or thin coat.

BURMESE STANDARD

SEAL POINT   *Scale*

COLOR 35

In maturity the body should be a rich, warm, seal brown without spotted areas or tabby markings. In adolescence color may be slightly lighter. Kittens are usually still lighter.

BODY AND TAIL 25

Medium in size. Not as long as the Siamese.

Legs, slim. Chest rounded. Tail medium long and straight; no kinks allowed.

HEAD AND EARS _____ 15

Head small, inclined to be round, with width between the eyes, narrowing to the muzzle. Allowance to be made for jowls in stud cat. Ears, erect, rather large, pricked, wide at base.

EYES _____ 15

Roundish, well-opened, alert in expression. Color ranging from golden to yellow.

COAT _____ 5

Glossy, fine in texture, *very short*, lying close to the body.

CONDITION _____ 5

Excellent physical condition. Not fat. Inclined to muscle.

UNDESIRABLE

Pale eye color; blue or odd eyes; tabby markings; white whether as scattered hairs or patches. Winners to be withheld from cats with bobbed, screw, kinked, or pom-pom tails.

RUSSIAN BLUE STANDARD

COLOR _____ 25

Bright blue, even throughout and free from tabby markings and shadings. There are various shades of blue, but the lighter or lavender blue is preferable. No white permissible.

COAT _____ 25

The fur should be very short, thick and very fine, standing up soft and silky like sealskin. Very different fur from that of any other breed of cat. It should not lie flat. The coat should be double, and the outer coat should have a distinct sheen.

BODY BUILD AND TAIL _____ 15

    Body, fine in bone, long, lithe and graceful outline and carriage with tail fairly long and tapering. Legs should be longer than those of the Domestic Short-Hair, and the feet should be small, neat, and well-rounded.

HEAD AND NECK _____ 15

    Skull should be flat. Face should be broad across the eyes; it looks wide because of the heavy fur. The nose is longer than that of the Persian but shorter than that of the Siamese. The neck is fairly long but looks short because of the thick fur.

EYES, COLOR AND SHAPE _____ 15

    Set rather wide apart, round, and vivid green in color.

EARS _____ 5

    Rather large, wide at the base, pointed at the tips rather than round, and with very little inside furnishings. Skin of ears thin and not too thickly covered with hair.

MANX STANDARD   *Scale*

TAILLESSNESS _____ 15

    Taillessness must be absolute in a show specimen. There should be a decided hollow at the end of the backbone where, in the ordinary cat, the tail would begin. Sometimes there is a slight rise at the end of the backbone where the tail would normally begin. While this rise is a fault and must be penalized, a stub, which is the first vertebra in a tail, is not allowed and winners must be withheld.

HEIGHT OF HINDQUARTERS _____ 15

    The hindquarters cannot be too high, resulting from very long back legs and much shorter forelegs. The hair will often be worn on the lower part of the back legs due to the fact that the Manx rests on this part as often as on the paws.

SHORTNESS OF BACK 15

General effect is that of a medium-sized, compact cat with sturdy bone and a very short back that arches from shoulders to haunches.

ROUNDNESS OF RUMP 10

The ideal would be as round as an orange.

DEPTH OF FLANK 10

The depth of flank is important, for together with the height of hindquarters, shortness of forelegs, shortness of back, and roundness of rump arises the hopping gait that is typical of the Manx.

DOUBLE COAT 10

Very soft double coat with a well-padded quality arising from the longer, open, outer coat and the thick close undercoat. The double coat gives the Manx the appearance of having a short, fluffy coat like that of a rabbit. This is essential.

HEAD AND EARS 10

Head should be round and large with prominent cheeks; muzzle broader than that of the Domestic Short-Hair but not of the snubby Persian type. The nose should be slightly longer than that of the Domestic Short-Hair, but there must be no suggestion of snipiness. Ears rather wide at the base, tapering slightly to a point.

COLOR AND MARKINGS 5

All colors of Manx are recognized, including ticked and mackerel tabbies, and parti-colored. Mackerel and ticked tabbies should be entered in the regular tabby classes. Winners not to be withheld for white "buttons" or "lockets."

EYES 5

Large, round, and full; color standard according to color of coat as in other breeds, but eye color should be of secondary consideration and should be taken into account only when all other points are equal.

CONDITION _____ 5

Good physical condition. Muscular—good flesh, but not fat.

All photographs by Mrs. Harriet Allen, Fredericksburg, Virginia and Three Lions, Inc., New York City. The Persian Cats on Pages 29-32 were taken with the cooperation of Mrs. Anita McDonald, Oceanside, N. Y., a member of the Empire Cat Club, N. Y. The Burmese and Abyssinian Cats were from Mrs. A. E. Rosenberg, St. Albans, N. Y. The Silver Tabby Cats were from Mr. John F. Luddy, Hazardville, Connecticut. The Angora was from Mr. Talat Beneir, Forest Hills, L. I., N. Y. The Manx Cat was from Mrs. George Heatherly, Harrisburg, Penna.